The World According to Whitbeck

By John V. Whitbeck

Five and Ten Press Inc.
Washington, D.C.
2005

This is a Black Sheep Book
published by Five and Ten Press Inc.

Black Sheep Books are sold by subscription
as well as individually.

First Edition

This is a limited edition of 600 copies.

To purchase a copy of this publication send a check for $10
payable to Five and Ten Press Inc. to the following address
(there is no charge for shipping and handling):
Five and Ten Press Inc.
3814 Livingston Street N.W.
Washington, D.C. 20015-2803

Cover artwork by Sean Whitbeck, age 11, a birthday present
to his father, the author, in 1995.

Cover design by Diahann Hill.

Printed in the United States of America
by Thomson-Shore, Inc.

Library of Congress Control Number: 2005922585

ISBN 1892379228

CONTENTS

ABOUT THE AUTHOR

John V. Whitbeck was born in 1946 in New York City. After graduating from Phillips Exeter Academy and Harvard College, where he majored in African History, he served as a Peace Corps teacher in Ethiopia and traveled for a year (principally in Africa) on a Sheldon Traveling Fellowship from Harvard before returning to Harvard Law School and then practicing law for three years in New York.

In 1976, his law firm, Sullivan & Cromwell, sent him on a two-year assignment to its Paris office. He never returned, becoming deeply involved with the Middle East and particularly with trying to help to achieve peace with some measure of justice for the Palestinians. He was in Madrid in October 1991 to contribute ideas for the Palestinian speeches delivered at the conference which launched the "peace process", in Cairo in April/May 1994 as a legal advisor to the Palestinian negotiating team which negotiated the Gaza/Jericho Withdrawal Agreement (the first "post-Oslo" agreement) with Israel and in a motel near Camp David in July 2000, when the "peace process" effectively ended, to be available to provide legal advice on any documents which emerged from the Arafat/Barak/Clinton summit. (None did.)

Since 1988, his articles on behalf of Middle East peace have been published more than 450 times in more than 70 different Arab, Israeli and international newspapers, magazines, journals and books, including, in the American press, in the Chicago Tribune, the Christian Science Monitor, the Dallas Morning News, the International Herald Tribune, the Los Angeles Times, Middle East Insight, Middle East Policy, The Nation, the Washington Post, the Washington Report on Middle East Affairs and the Washington Times.

This volume contains all of his articles published during the period from the assumption of power by George W. Bush and Ariel Sharon in early 2001 through the end of 2004, preceded by two reminders of a far more optimistic era – late publications of his "Two States, One Holy Land" framework for peace (published 40 times, in various lengths and languages, between January 1988, one month after the start of the first intifada, and 2000) and his "condominium solution" for sharing Jerusalem in a context of peace and reconciliation (published 49 times, in various lengths and languages, between 1994 and 2000).

While the "peace process" was still active and hopeful, he traveled frequently to Israel and Palestine and spoke at numerous conferences in America, Europe and the Middle East to try to promote his proposals for Middle East peace. In November 1993, two months after the "Oslo" Declaration of Principles was signed on the White House lawn, his "Two States, One Holy Land" framework for peace was the subject of a three-day conference in Cairo, attended by 24 prominent Israelis and Palestinians, including four Knesset members and Palestinian Foreign Minister Nabeel Shaath, under the sponsorship of The Middle East Institute (Washington).

Prior to the dissolution of the Soviet Union, when the world comprised only 213 countries (counting both sovereign states and non-sovereign territories with populations of at least 5000), he had traveled in all of them.

Since 1999, he has commuted between Jeddah, where he practices Saudi Arabian law, and Paris, where his wife and four sons live.

TWO STATES, ONE HOLY LAND

This proposed framework for peace was published 40 times, in various lengths and in the Arabic, Dutch, English, French, German and Hebrew languages, between 1988 and 2000. It was first published on January 25, 1988 by the *Los Angeles Times*. The version below appeared in the August 20, 1999 issue of *Middle East International* (London).

As the Israeli-Palestinian peace process struggles to move forward again, what is most sadly missing is any compelling vision of how a Holy Land at peace could be structured in the new millennium so as to enhance not only the physical security of Israelis and the human dignity of Palestinians but also the quality of day-to-day life for both peoples.

While Yitzhak Rabin never revealed his vision (if any) of what "permanent status" might actually look like (even, according to her own admission, to his wife), Ehud Barak has given a glimpse of his own vision. It is based on the principle that "tall fences make good neighbors" and aspires to reduce the number of Palestinians working in Israel to zero. It features a 47-kilometer-long elevated highway between the Gaza Strip and the West Bank – elevated so as to prevent any Israeli-Palestinian contact or contamination. Its key word is "separation" (*apartheid* in Afrikaans). It is a profoundly depressing vision, far from the goal of a "historic reconciliation" proclaimed in the Declaration of Principles so optimistically signed on the White House lawn in September 1993.

Can Israelis and Palestinians really do no better than this? Is there really no middle ground between "Greater Israel" and *apartheid*? Or might it still be possible to blend the practical and psychological necessity of a two-state solution with some of the best aspects of a humane one-state solution to produce a vision of a possible future so bright that both Israelis and Palestinians would be inspired to act on their hopes and dreams rather than their memories and fears and to seize this future

3

together and make it a reality?

Sharing the Holy Land is not a zero-sum game in which any development advantageous to one side must be disadvantageous to the other. One can envisage a society in which, by separating political and voting rights from economic, social and residential rights in a negotiated settlement, both the legitimate national aspirations of Palestinians and the legitimate security interests of Israelis could be simultaneously satisfied.

The non-negotiable minimum for both Israelis and Palestinians is their own self-determination as peoples and nations, that they can have a state of their own in the land that both love, including at least some share of Jerusalem, and that never again will anyone else govern them. This is not impossible. The Holy Land could be a two-state "confederation", a single economic and social unit encompassing two sovereign states and one Holy City. Jerusalem could be an Israeli-Palestinian "condominium", forming an undivided part of both states, being the capital of both states and being administered by an umbrella municipal council and local district councils.

All current residents of the Holy Land could be given the choice of Israeli or Palestinian citizenship, thus determining which state's passport they would carry and in which state's national elections they would vote. All citizens of either state could vote in municipal elections where they actually live, a matter of particular relevance to Israeli Arabs opting for Palestinian citizenship and to Israeli settlers choosing to continue to live in Palestine. Each state could have its own "law of return" conferring citizenship and residential rights within that state on persons not currently resident in the Holy Land.

Borders would have to be drawn on maps but would not have to exist on the ground. The free, non-discriminatory movement of people and products within the Holy Land could be a fundamental principle subject only to one major exception: to ensure that each state would always maintain its national character, the right to residence in each Holy Land state could be limited to that state's citizens, to citizens of the other state

4

residing there on an agreed future date and to their descendants. (In this way, deeply felt principles could be maintained. Israelis could have the right to live in all of Eretz Israel – but not *all* Israelis in *all* of Eretz Israel. Similarly, Palestinians could have the right to live in all of historic Palestine – but not *all* Palestinians in *all* of historic Palestine.) A common currency (perhaps printed in Hebrew on one side and Arabic on the other) could be issued by a common central bank.

To ease Israeli security concerns, the Palestinian state could be fully demilitarized, with only Palestinian police allowed to bear arms within its territory. As an essential counterpart to the absence of border controls within the Holy Land, Israel could conduct its own immigration controls, at the same time that Palestine conducts its immigration controls, at the frontiers of the Palestinian state with Egypt and Jordan, with any non-Palestinian visitors restricted to the Palestinian state by the Israeli authorities facing penalties if found in Israel. The settlement agreement could be guaranteed by the United Nations and relevant states, with international tribunals to arbitrate disputes regarding compliance with its terms.

The status of Jerusalem poses the toughest problem for any settlement plan, causing many to assume, for this reason alone, that no settlement acceptable to both sides can ever be reached. When the UN General Assembly adopted Resolution 181 in 1947, it addressed the problem by suggesting an international status for Jerusalem, with neither the Jewish state nor the Arab state to have sovereignty over the city. Yet joint undivided sovereignty, while rare, is not without precedent.

Chandigarh is the joint undivided capital of two Indian states. For half a century, Sudan was a condominium of Britain and Egypt, officially named "Anglo-Egyptian Sudan". For more than 70 years, the Pacific Islands state of Vanuatu (formerly the New Hebrides Condominium) was under the joint undivided sovereignty of Britain and France. For more than 700 years, until a 1993 constitutional revision, the Principality of Andorra was under the joint undivided sovereignty of French and Spanish "co-princes". In March 1999, the arbitrator appointed

5

by the International Court of Justice ruled that the contested Bosnian municipality of Brcko should be a condominium shared by Bosnia's Serb Republic and its Muslim-Croat Federation. As a joint capital, Jerusalem could have Israeli government offices principally in its western sector, Palestinian government offices principally in its eastern sector and municipal offices in both. A system of districts or French-style *arrondissements* could bring municipal government closer to the different communities in the city. To the extent that either state wished to control persons or goods passing into it from the other state, this could be done at the points of exit from, rather than the points of entry to, Jerusalem. In a context of peace, particularly one coupled with economic union, the need for such controls would be minimal.

In a sense, Jerusalem can be viewed as a cake which could be sliced either vertically or horizontally. Either way, the Palestinians would get a share of the cake, but, while most Israelis could never voluntarily swallow a vertical slice, they might just be able to swallow a horizontal slice. (Indeed, by doing so, Israel would finally achieve international recognition of Jerusalem as its capital.) Jerusalem is both a municipality on the ground and a symbol in hearts and minds. Undivided but shared in this way, Jerusalem could be a symbol of reconciliation and hope for Jews, Muslims, Christians and the world as a whole.

Such a framework would address in ways advantageous to both sides the three principal practical problems on the road to peace – Jerusalem (through joint sovereignty over an undivided city), settlers (through a separation of citizenship rights from residential rights in a regime of free access to the entire Holy Land for all citizens of both states under which no one would be compelled to move) and borders (through a structure of relations between the two states so open and non-threatening that the precise placement of borders would no longer be such a contentious issue and the pre-1967 borders – subject only to the expanded borders of Jerusalem, under joint sovereignty – might well be acceptable to most Israelis, as they

6

would certainly be to most Palestinians).

For Jewish Israelis, the threat of one day living in a state with a majority of Arab voters or an inescapable resemblance to pre-1990 South Africa would be replaced by the assurance of living in a democratic state with fewer Arab voters than today. The Israelis' security would be enhanced by assuaging, rather than continuing to aggravate, the Palestinians' grievances. By escaping from the role (so tragic in light of Jewish history) of oppressors and enforcers of injustice, Israel would save its soul and its dreams.

For all Palestinians, human dignity would be restored. They would cease to be a people treated (and not only by Israelis) as pariahs uniquely unworthy of basic human rights. For those in exile, an internationally accepted Palestinian citizenship, a Palestinian passport and a right to return, if only to visit, would have enormous significance. And if the Palestinians themselves accepted a settlement, few, if any, Arab states would continue to reject Israel. If a Palestinian flag were peacefully raised over Palestinian government offices in Jerusalem, few Arab eyes would still see Israel through a veil of hatred. The immovable obstacle to a lasting region-wide peace would have been removed.

While implementation of such a framework for peace would be relatively simple, its acceptance would require a moral, spiritual and psychological transformation from both Israelis and Palestinians. Yet, given the decades of hatred, bitterness and distrust, *any* settlement would require such a transformation. Precisely because such a transformation would be so difficult, it is far more likely to be achieved if both peoples can be inspired by a truly compelling vision of a new society of peaceful coexistence, mutual respect and human dignity, in which both peoples are winners, than if they are left to contemplate painful programs for a new partition and an angry separation in which both peoples must regard themselves, to a considerable degree, as admitting defeat.

Israelis, Palestinians and the true friends of both must now raise their sights beyond the minutiae of the Wye

Memorandum and pursue a compelling vision of a society so much better than the status quo that both Israelis and Palestinians are inspired to accept in their hearts and minds that peace is both desirable and attainable, that the Holy Land *can* be shared, that a winner-take-all approach produces only losers, that both Israelis and Palestinians must be winners or both will continue to be losers and that there is a common destination at which both peoples would be satisfied to arrive and to live together.

Peace is unimaginable on any other basis.

SHARING JERUSALEM: THE CONDOMINIUM SOLUTION

This proposed solution for the status of Jerusalem, a fundamental component of the "Two States, One Holy Land" framework for peace, was published as a separate article 49 times, in various lengths and in the Arabic, English, French, German, Hebrew and Spanish languages, between 1994 and 2000. It was first published on April 7, 1994 in *Al-Quds* (Jerusalem). The version below appeared in the February 2000 issue of the quarterly journal *Middle East Policy* (Washington). *Middle East Policy* also published an earlier version in its Fall 1994 issue.

There will never be a durable peace in the Middle East without a settlement of the Israeli-Palestinian conflict acceptable both to most Israelis and to most Palestinians. That is a fact. There will also never be a lasting settlement of the Israeli-Palestinian conflict without a solution to the status of Jerusalem acceptable both to most Israelis and to most Palestinians. That is also a fact, one which, as the September 2000 deadline for reaching a permanent status agreement approaches, is increasingly difficult (and dangerous) for anyone to ignore.

It is still widely assumed that no such solution exists. As a result, doubts, distrust and even despair are still widespread on both sides. Many people, on both sides as well as abroad, have no faith in the current "peace process" and no desire to become involved in it and to help it to succeed because they see at the end of the road a great immovable boulder named Jerusalem which they believe condemns any "peace process" to ultimate and inevitable failure.

Nothing is more likely to revive a constructive confidence in the eventual success of the "peace process" and to accelerate the essential moral, spiritual and psychological transformation toward a cooperative, rather than a confrontational, view of the future of the Middle East than a prompt recognition that a solution to the status of Jerusalem *does* exist. Fortunately, there is one solution which has a real chance of being acceptable both to most Israelis and to most Palestinians.

When Israelis and Palestinians speak about Jerusalem, they are not simply laying out negotiating positions. Jerusalem has too tight a grip on hearts and minds. Their repeated and virtually unanimous positions must be taken seriously. If one accepts, as one must, that no Israeli government could ever accept a redivision of Jerusalem, and if one accepts, as one must, that no Palestinian leadership could ever accept a permanent status solution which gave the Palestinian State (and, through it, the Arab and Muslim worlds) no share of sovereignty in Jerusalem, then only one solution is conceivable – joint sovereignty over an undivided city. In the context of a two-state solution, Jerusalem could form an undivided part of both states, be the capital of both states and be administered by an umbrella municipal council and local district councils. In the proper terminology of international law, the city would be a "condominium" of Israel and Palestine.

Joint undivided sovereignty, while rare, is not without precedent. Chandigarh is the joint undivided capital of two neighboring Indian states, Haryana and Punjab. For half a century prior to its independence in 1956, Sudan was a condominium of Britain and Egypt, officially named "Anglo-Egyptian Sudan". For more than 70 years, the Pacific nation of Vanuatu (formerly the New Hebrides Condominium) was under the joint undivided sovereignty of Britain and France, with each resident free to choose whether to be subject to British laws or French laws. For more than 700 years, until a 1993 constitutional revision, the Principality of Andorra was under the joint undivided sovereignty of French and Spanish "co-princes" (since 1607, the head of the French state and the Bishop of Seo de Urgel) while its administration has in recent years been entrusted to an elected General Council. (Since 1993, the co-princes have served as co-heads of state of a conventionally sovereign UN member state rather than as joint sovereigns.) In March 1999, the arbitrator appointed by the International Court of Justice ruled that the contested Bosnian municipality of

Brcko should be a condominium shared by Bosnia's Serb Republic and its Muslim-Croat Federation, with its own local administration.

As a joint capital, Jerusalem could have Israeli government offices principally in its western sector, Palestinian government offices principally in its eastern sector and municipal offices in both. A system of districts or French-style *arrondissements* could bring municipal administration closer to the different communities in the city (including the ultra-orthodox Jewish community). To the extent that either state wished to control persons or goods entering it from the other state, this could be done at the points of exit from, rather than the points of entry to, Jerusalem. In a context of peace, particularly one coupled with economic union, the need for such controls would be minimal.

In a sense, Jerusalem can be viewed as a cake which could be sliced either vertically or horizontally. Either way, the Palestinians would get a share of the cake, but, while most Israelis could never voluntarily swallow a vertical slice, they might just be able to swallow a horizontal slice. Indeed, by doing so, Israel would finally achieve international recognition of Jerusalem as its capital.

Jerusalem is both a municipality on the ground and a symbol in hearts and minds. Undivided but shared in this way, Jerusalem could be a symbol of reconciliation and hope for Jews, Muslims, Christians and the world as a whole. Furthermore, since a city needs no army but only police, Jerusalem could also be fully demilitarized, finally becoming the "City of Peace" which all three religions have long proclaimed it to be.

Among peace-oriented Israelis and Palestinians there is a broad consensus that, in any permanent status solution, Jerusalem should remain *physically* undivided. However, there is no consensus on how the problem of sovereignty should be solved. That issue remains almost too hot to handle. Indeed, it is a bit like death. Everyone knows that it is at the end of the road, but virtually no one wants to talk about it because virtually no one can see any solution or happy ending.

The issue of sovereignty over Jerusalem is such an emotional one, and the consensus within each community behind its own uncompromising position is (or is at least *proclaimed* and *perceived* to be) so nearly universal, that there is no incentive for those within the communities directly engaged to stick their necks out by proposing any original or unorthodox ideas on the subject. Even today, any Israeli or Palestinian who sought publicly to promote a compromise solution to the issue of sovereignty over Jerusalem which he honestly believed could be acceptable to the other side would risk being castigated as a traitor or a heretic by the vocal majority of his compatriots or coreligionists.

When the Israeli Moshe Amirav and the Palestinian Hanna Siniora published their courageous and thoughtful joint article entitled "Jerusalem: Resolving the Unresolvable" during the winter of 1991/92, they did not shy away from making controversial proposals, notably including their calls for parity between Israelis and Palestinians in all aspects of civil, political and religious life in the city, for a four-fold expansion of the area within the municipal boundaries so as to equalize the size of the two communities and for strict "immigration" controls to maintain this demographic balance. However, even they did not dare to address directly the question of sovereignty, "so as to appear non-threatening to Israelis", but sought instead to make it "manageable by breaking it down into its various components" and tackling each one separately.

"Joint undivided sovereignty" is a concept which even highly intelligent people are often unable to comprehend. Perhaps, paradoxically, it is too simple to be easily understood. While sovereignty is commonly viewed as the state-level equivalent of title or ownership, joint undivided ownership of land or a house (between husband and wife or, through inheritance, among distant cousins) is scarcely uncommon. Such joint undivided ownership is clear as a matter of law and comprehensible as a matter of practice. It is up to the joint owners to determine how their common property is to be *administered.*

In seeking a solution to the status of Jerusalem, it is essential to distinguish between *sovereignty* and municipal *administration.* Questions of municipal administration, including the division of authorities between an umbrella municipal council and local district councils, exist for any sizable city, regardless of any questions of sovereignty. In Jerusalem's case, it would clearly be desirable, employing the European Union's principle of "subsidiarity", to devolve as many aspects of municipal governance as possible to the district council level, reserving to the umbrella municipal council only those major matters which can only be administered efficiently at a city-wide level (potentially very few matters, since, notwithstanding the election of a new Greater London Authority and a mayor this May, London has continued to function quite efficiently with only local district councils and with no umbrella municipal council since the Greater London Council was abolished in 1986). Since there are currently no integrated neighborhoods in Jerusalem, assuring that Israelis are subject to Israeli administration, and Palestinians to Palestinian administration, at the district council level would present no practical problems.

If the devolution of authority to the district council level was broad and deep, the potentially inflammatory issue of the percentage representations of the two communities on the umbrella municipal council would be much less problematic. If elected district councils named their own representatives to the umbrella municipal council, a more technocratic and less demagogic style of municipal government might be possible. If the percentage representations of the two communities, through their respective municipal districts, on the umbrella municipal council were fixed at an agreed level (whatever that level might be) and made impervious to subsequent demographic changes within the municipal boundaries, the issue of post-peace "immigration" of Israelis and Palestinians into Jerusalem would become a non-issue and the purely political motivation for building more Jewish residential districts in expanded East

Jerusalem or for expanding the current municipal boundaries even further to incorporate additional Jewish population centers would evaporate.

While municipal administration involves numerous practical questions, sovereignty over Jerusalem is fundamentally a symbolic, psychological and virtually theological question. Symbolism, psychology and theology are *extraordinarily* important in connection with Jerusalem (more so than with any other city on earth), but it is important to recognize that this is the nature of the question. An "internationalization" of the city, with neither Israel nor Palestine possessing sovereignty, was recommended in 1947 by UN General Assembly Resolution 181. This recommendation has never been revoked and continues to enjoy significant international support and moral authority. However, "internationalization" would serve no useful *symbolic* or *psychological* purpose for those most directly involved and thus cannot be a realistic option today.

Assigning sovereignty over an undivided city both to Israel and to Palestine should satisfy to the maximum degree possible the symbolic and psychological needs of both Israelis and Palestinians. It could also produce profound positive psychological benefits for the quality of "life after peace" by requiring in spirit and in practice a sharing of the city and cooperation with "the other" rather than a new partitioning of the city and mere toleration of "the other" or the continuing domination of one people over another, with all the poisonous frictions which such a domination inevitably provokes.

One of the strengths and beauties of joint undivided sovereignty, and a potential advantage in making it acceptable to both peoples and to their leaderships, is that it would not require either Israel or Palestine to renounce sovereignty over any territory over which it has asserted sovereignty. The State of Palestine asserts sovereignty only over those Palestinian lands conquered and occupied in 1967. Of those lands, the State of Israel asserts sovereignty only over expanded East Jerusalem. Under a "condominium" solution, in the only place where current sovereignty claims overlap, sovereignty would overlap and be shared. To repeat, *neither Israel nor Palestine would have to renounce sovereignty over any territory over which it has asserted sovereignty.* Potentially intractable negotiations over where to draw international borders through and even within Jerusalem would be completely avoided, since the city would not be divided but shared.

Israelis should ask themselves what (if anything) they would actually be giving up in accepting joint undivided sovereignty over Jerusalem. Approximately 70 percent of the city's residents are now Israelis, and Palestinian residents already have the right to vote in municipal elections. That would not change. Put most simply, all Israel would have to do is say this: "United Jerusalem, within the expanded boundaries which we have unilaterally established, is the eternal capital of Israel ... *but,* in order to make peace possible, we accept that it is also the capital of Palestine." That's all. While, today, only Costa Rica and El Salvador even recognize *West* Jerusalem as Israel's capital, and no country recognizes Israeli sovereignty over East Jerusalem, if Israel adopted such a position and implemented it with Palestinian consent, virtually all countries would promptly recognize *united* Jerusalem as Israel's capital. Embassies would move there. Is this really so awful and unthinkable for Israelis? Is this really impossible?

There is a widespread misconception among Israelis that, under the *status quo,* Israel possesses sovereignty over expanded East Jerusalem. It does not. It possesses administrative control. A country can acquire administrative control by force of arms. It can acquire sovereignty only with the consent of the international community.

When Iraq conquered Kuwait, it asserted sovereignty over it. No other country recognized that claim. For the next seven months, Iraq's position in Kuwait – effective administrative control coupled with an unrecognized claim to sovereignty – was, as a matter of international law, effectively indistinguishable from Israel's position in expanded East Jerusalem today. (Indonesia's position in East Timor was, until recently, similar, and Morocco's position in Western Sahara remains similar.) Israel has possessed and exercised administrative control over expanded East Jerusalem for more than three decades. To this day, not one of the world's other 192 sovereign states has recognized its claim to sovereignty.

Israel could retain administrative control over expanded East Jerusalem indefinitely. That is a question of military strength and political will. However, it is most unlikely that it will ever acquire sovereignty over expanded East Jerusalem unless it agrees to a permanent solution to the status of Jerusalem based on joint undivided sovereignty over the entire city. That is a question of law. Indeed, since the right of a country to declare any part of its sovereign territory to be its capital is not contested, the refusal of virtually all countries to recognize West Jerusalem as Israel's capital and the maintenance of virtually all embassies (even including the American embassy) in Tel Aviv is striking evidence of the refusal of the international community, pending an agreed permanent solution to the status of Jerusalem, to concede that *any* part of the city is Israel's sovereign territory.

A vivid example of the firm and unequivocal position of the international community is provided by UN General Assembly Resolution 53/37, adopted on December 2, 1998 by a vote of 149-1 (with the United States abstaining), in which "The General Assembly ... *Determines* that the decision of Israel to impose its laws, jurisdiction and administration on the Holy City of Jerusalem is illegal and therefore null and void and has no validity whatsoever." In May 1996, the world's view of the legal status of Jerusalem was concisely summarized by then British Foreign Secretary Malcolm Rifkind: "Britain made clear many years ago, as did the international community, that it considered Israel to be in military occupation of East Jerusalem and to have only *de facto* authority over West Jerusalem."

A clearer understanding of what the legal *status quo* regarding Jerusalem really is could make Israeli public opinion less reflexively resistant to contemplating any modification of that *status quo*, even in return for peace.

It is clear that joint undivided sovereignty is not the first choice of either Israelis or Palestinians. Exclusive Israeli sovereignty over the whole city would clearly be the first choice of most Israelis, but this is equally clearly unacceptable not only to Palestinians but also to the Arab and Muslim countries with which Israel wishes to have normal diplomatic and economic relations and which would accept any permanent status terms which the Palestinians might accept *except that one*, as well as to significant segments of the international community beyond the Arab and Muslim worlds. The Basic Agreement signed at the Vatican on February 15 between the Holy See and the Palestine Liberation Organization is noteworthy in this regard. It declares "that an equitable solution for the issue of Jerusalem, based on international resolutions, is fundamental for a just and lasting peace in the Middle East, and that unilateral decisions and actions altering the specific character and status of Jerusalem are morally and legally unacceptable" and calls "for a special statute for Jerusalem, internationally guaranteed, which should safeguard", among other things, "the equality before the law of the three monotheistic religions and their institutions and followers in the City".

A division of sovereignty and a redivision of administrative control strictly in accordance with the pre-1967 border (and hence with international law and UN Security Council Resolution 242) would clearly be the first choice of most Palestinians, but, particularly in light of the presence of the Western Wall, enormous Jewish settlements and even a slight Israeli population majority in expanded East Jerusalem, this is equally clearly inconceivable from the Israeli standpoint. (While expanded East Jerusalem is effectively indistinguishable from the other occupied territories as a matter of international law, it is most certainly distinguishable and distinguished as a matter of Israeli domestic law and, most importantly, in Israeli public perception.)

These irreconcilable "first choice options" must, logically, be discarded by all who truly wish to achieve peace. Such people should be searching now for a mutually acceptable "best second choice". If one accepts the two premises that no

Israeli government could ever accept a redivision of Jerusalem and that no Palestinian leadership (and certainly not the Arab and Muslim worlds) could ever accept a permanent status solution which gave the Palestinian State no share of sovereignty in Jerusalem, then, as a matter of pure logic, joint undivided sovereignty is the *only* possible second choice if peace is ever to be achieved. However, even if the first premise were *untrue* (there being no reason to believe that the second premise might be untrue) and a division of sovereignty in Jerusalem *could* be agreed upon, joint undivided sovereignty might still be the best possible second choice for both Israelis and Palestinians.

Any solution to the status of Jerusalem, like any solution to the Israeli-Palestinian conflict as a whole, must have two characteristics if it is to produce a durable peace. It must be workable, and it must, at least in some measure, be inspirational. If a potential solution is technically workable but fails to inspire hearts and minds, it is unlikely to succeed. If a potential solution inspires hearts and minds but is unworkable on the ground, it too is unlikely to succeed. In thinking both about Jerusalem and about the Israeli-Palestinian conflict as a whole, all who truly wish to achieve peace should be searching for solutions which are both workable and inspirational.

The most obvious question regarding joint undivided sovereignty is "What law would apply?". The question tends to be posed on the assumption that it is unanswerable and that the "condominium" solution for Jerusalem, notwithstanding its inspirational aspects, would be unworkable in practice. In fact, there is not just one potentially workable answer to this question but several.

One approach would be for Jerusalem to have its own distinct body of laws, neither wholly Israeli nor wholly Palestinian and applicable within its boundaries to all who are present there. There is an appealing surface simplicity to this approach, which would have been virtually unavoidable had the city been "internationalized" pursuant to the United Nations' 1947 partition formula. However, as a practical matter, such a body of laws could only be based on those currently in force in the city as subsequently modified by the umbrella municipal council or, perhaps, by agreement between the Israeli and Palestinian states. Consequently, Jerusalem's laws would, for the foreseeable future, be virtually indistinguishable from Israel's laws (draining joint undivided sovereignty of most of its content in Palestinian eyes), while the umbrella municipal council, best kept technocratic, could become highly politicized. While the "Jerusalem law" approach could be workable, there are better approaches.

A second approach would be to apply Israeli law in every Israeli-majority district as fully as though that district were an integral part of Israel alone and to apply Palestinian law in every Palestinian-majority district as fully as though that district were an integral part of Palestine alone. This is the approach called for in the "scattered sovereignty" model developed in recent years by the Israel/Palestine Center for Research and Information (IPCRI) in Jerusalem, which would draw international borders around every currently existing village, neighborhood or settlement in expanded East Jerusalem and put each of them under the exclusive sovereignty of one of the two states (thereby requiring *both* Israel and Palestine to renounce sovereignty over territory over which they have asserted sovereignty). This approach would be entirely appropriate if a "scattered sovereignty" model were implemented and would even be potentially workable if a "condominium" solution were implemented. However, it is conceptually inconsistent with the uplifting vision of a single undivided city serving as the capital of both states, would produce practical results which both peoples would consider undesirable and would tend to lock in indefinitely the pervasive segregation of the city's existing neighborhoods.

A third approach, more supple and subtle, is the most promising one. Rather than seeking to establish a distinct body of laws for Jerusalem or providing a purely territorial basis for determining whether Israeli or Palestinian law applies, one can envision a more flexible system pursuant to which the law applicable in any specific instance would depend on the subject matter, the parties involved and the municipal district in which the issue or dispute arises.

Legal experts negotiating in good faith while keeping in mind three broad areas of law (civil, criminal and personal) and two potential bases for jurisdiction (personal and territorial) should be fully capable of agreeing upon appropriate choices of applicable law and jurisdiction based on objective, non-discriminatory and results-oriented criteria. Their task would be to agree upon those situations in which the personal/national element would control, those in which the territorial element would control, those in which an agreed "tiebreaker" would decide and those (if any) in which resort to a "mixed court" would be necessary.

A few examples should help to clarify how such a flexible legal system would work. Both sides might well agree that the personal/national element should control in all personal law matters (most notably marriage, divorce and inheritance), with Israeli law applicable to Israelis and Palestinian law applicable to Palestinians regardless of the municipal district in which they live. They might also agree that the territorial element should control in matters relating to property, with the prevailing law of the municipal district where the property is located being applicable, regardless of the citizenships of the parties involved.

In the area of contractual disputes, it might be agreed that Israeli law should apply to disputes between Israelis and Palestinian law to disputes between Palestinians, with the territorial element serving as a "tiebreaker" in any contractual dispute between an Israeli Jerusalemite and a Palestinian Jerusalemite where there was no explicit "choice of law" clause in a written contract. It might also be agreed that the territorial element should control in cases of theft, with the accused thief being deemed to have made his own effective "choice of law".

The most difficult and highly charged situation would probably involve a murder within the municipal boundaries of Jerusalem. There would almost certainly be agreement that, if both victim and suspect were Israeli, Israeli law should apply even if the crime occurred in a Palestinian-majority district and that, if both victim and suspect were Palestinian, Palestinian law should apply even if the crime occurred in an Israeli-majority district. If victim and suspect were of different citizenships, a "tiebreaker" would be needed. It is not certain that a territorial "tiebreaker" would be acceptable to both sides or, indeed, to either side. It is possible that it could be agreed that the law of the suspect's citizenship or the law of the victim's citizenship should apply. It is also possible that no "tiebreaker" could be agreed upon for cases of murder and perhaps for some other difficult and highly charged situations as well.

The last resort would be a "mixed court", composed of one Israeli judge, one Palestinian judge and one international judge accepted in advance by both governments. There is a history of "mixed courts" operating in diverse places (including the New Hebrides Condominium) and in difficult circumstances during the nineteenth and twentieth centuries and dispensing a reasonable degree of justice. Ideally, they would not be needed in Jerusalem. However, if, in one or more instances, no objective criteria could be agreed upon for determining whose law and jurisdiction would be applicable, then "mixed courts" would be the alternative to no solution at all.

The results-oriented balancing process necessary to agree upon such a legal structure for a Jerusalem equitably shared by both peoples and their states may seem complicated at first glance. However, the practical results in the lives of Jerusalem's residents would almost certainly be better than under a more rigid system, and the fluidity of such a legal system would itself emphasize the unique nature of Jerusalem as the undivided capital of two sovereign states. Agreeing upon the relevant practical criteria would be infinitely easier than rolling aside the symbolic and psychological boulder of the issue of sovereignty. The "condominium" solution is a workable solution.

The "condominium" solution has the advantage of being consistent with both the letter and the spirit of the formal American position on Jerusalem, which urges that the city

21

should remain undivided and that its permanent status should be determined through negotiations between Israelis and Palestinians. It is even consistent (at least up to a point) with the letter (if not the spirit) of the long-standing formal Israeli position, as restated by the late Prime Minister Yitzhak Rabin during a joint press conference with President Bill Clinton in Jerusalem on October 27, 1994: "Jerusalem must remain united under the sovereignty of Israel." Whether a "united" or "undivided" Jerusalem could be *shared* under the sovereignty of Israel *and Palestine* has not yet been formally addressed, although the word "exclusive" has recently entered Israeli political discourse in apparent anticipation of such a possibility.

The "condominium" solution is further from the traditional Palestinian position with its steadfast reliance on "international legitimacy", international law and UN resolutions. With an exceptionally weak hand to play in terms of military strength and power politics, Palestinians have long drawn comfort from their certainty that international law is on their side – and it is on their side, overwhelmingly so. (Indeed, the "maximalist" Palestinian negotiating position is nothing more nor less than full compliance with international law and relevant UN resolutions.) However, the decisions to enter into the 1993 Declaration of Principles and its various follow-up agreements reflect a mature acceptance of the brutal truth that a strong position under international law does not alone ensure even the slightest measure of justice. Agreeing not to insist on their strong position under international law with respect to expanded East Jerusalem and to share sovereignty in the only part of the former Palestine Mandate where current sovereignty claims overlap (as well as in West Jerusalem) may be the practical price which Palestinians must pay for successfully asserting Palestine's strong position under international law and Palestinian sovereignty with respect to all other Palestinian lands conquered and occupied in 1967.

Indeed, since mid-1995, President Yasser Arafat and other members of the Palestinian leadership have given increasingly clear indications that they are susceptible to the

22

charms and practical merits of the "condominium" solution and favorably disposed toward it. Faisal Husseini, in charge of the "Jerusalem file" for the Palestinian leadership, has stated that, during permanent status negotiations, "we will insist that the negotiations cover all of Jerusalem (including West Jerusalem occupied by Israel in 1948) and not only East Jerusalem." In a speech at Harvard University's Kennedy School of Government in October 1995, President Arafat asked, "Why not Jerusalem as the capital of two states, with no Berlin wall? United, open, coexistence, living together." The audience rose for a standing ovation.

Realistically, there are only three alternative endings to the search for Israeli-Palestinian peace: (1) Israel and Palestine agree on a basis for dividing Jerusalem, and peace is achieved on that basis; (2) Israel and Palestine agree to share an undivided Jerusalem, and peace is achieved on that basis; or (3) Israel and Palestine fail to agree on Jerusalem's status, and there is no peace. All the major Israeli political parties, as well as Prime Minister Ehud Barak personally, have ruled out dividing Jerusalem in the most categorical conceivable terms. In November 1997, even the ruling council of the Meretz Party, ostensibly the most left-wing and peace-oriented of the predominantly Jewish parties in the Knesset, decisively rejected a motion in favor of divided sovereignty in a physically undivided Jerusalem.

That leaves only the second and third alternatives – sharing and no peace – a sobering reality which should, logically, stimulate interest among peace-seekers in exploring the potential of the "condominium" solution and in trying to convince Israeli public opinion that the Holy City (as well as the Holy Land) *can* be shared, that a winner-take-all approach produces only losers, that both Israelis and Palestinians must be winners or both will continue to be losers and that there is a common destination at which both peoples would be satisfied to arrive and to live together in peace.

A century after the First Zionist Congress was held in 1897 and half a century after Israel was established in 1948,

Israelis concerned about their future might well look back at the vision for Jerusalem of Theodor Herzl, the founding father of Zionism: "We'll simply extraterritorialize Jerusalem, which will then belong to nobody and yet to everybody, the holy place common to the adherents of all faiths, the great condominium of culture and morality." Herzl's dream of a Jewish State was wildly impractical at the time, but it existed half a century later. Whether its people ever enjoy peace and security may well depend on whether they can grasp the visionary practicality of Herzl's own recognition that what neither people of the Holy Land could ever relinquish or renounce must therefore be shared.

If Israelis and Palestinians can agree - and soon – that a mutually acceptable solution for the status of Jerusalem *does exist*, all the other pieces in the delicate peace puzzle could still fall into place and the actual achievement of a durable Middle East peace would at once become possible. Without a mutually acceptable solution for the status of Jerusalem, everything will fall apart. That cannot be permitted to happen.

The road to "interim self-rule" may have started in Gaza and Jericho and been extended to other West Bank cities, but any road to peace must start in Jerusalem.

NO TO NON-BELLIGERENCY – YES TO PEACE

PUBLICATIONS:

April 19, 2001 – Asharq Al-Awsat (London)
April 19 – Jordan Times (Amman)
April 20 – Al-Quds (Jerusalem)
April 21 – Arab News (Jeddah)
April 30 – Daily Star (Beirut)
May 4 – Jerusalem Times
May 4 – Middle East International (London)
May 17 – Al-Ahram Weekly (Cairo)
June 2001 – Le Dossier Euro-Arabe (Paris)
September 9 – Sunday Mail (Nicosia)

When, almost ten years ago, Yitzhak Shamir lost his bid for reelection as Israel's prime minister, he gave a remarkably frank interview to the Israeli newspaper *Ma'ariv*. Mr. Shamir stated that, if reelected, he would have dragged out Israeli-Palestinian negotiations for ten years while settling a further half a million Jews in the occupied Palestinian territories. (Actually, he referred to "souls" rather than to "Jews" and to "Judea, Samaria and Gaza" rather than to the occupied Palestinian territories, but everyone knew what he meant.) He thereby made clear that it was never *his* intention that the "peace process" launched at the 1991 Madrid Peace Conference should, in fact, lead to peace.

It should now be sadly clear that Mr. Shamir's electoral defeat changed nothing. His spirit lived on in Yitzhak Rabin, Shimon Peres, Benjamin Netanyahu and Ehud Barak. While a full half a million Jews have not settled in the occupied Palestinian territories since the "peace process" began in Madrid, the number of settlers living there has approximately doubled during this period, and all of Mr. Shamir's successors have demonstrated, in deeds if not in words, that their only

25

interest in the "peace process" was in the "process" (intended to keep the rest of the world off their back while they dug in deeper in the occupied Palestinian territories) rather than in "peace".

Until Ariel Sharon, that is. He at least has the merit of honesty in having formally dropped any pretense of seeking peace with Palestine. He has made clear, with support from his soulmate and Foreign Minister Shimon Peres and to apparent international indifference, that all he is interested in negotiating with the Palestinians is a "long-term non-belligerency agreement".

What precisely would a "non-belligerency agreement" between an occupying power and an occupied people signify? "Non-belligerency" may sound like a close cousin of "peace", but its essence could not be more different. In the Israeli-Palestinian context, it would signify Palestinian acquiescence in the continuing illegal occupation of the Palestinian lands conquered in 1967 and Palestinian renunciation of the internationally recognized right to resist occupation. Where will one find the Palestinian who would be interested in even discussing such a thing?

Nevertheless, the near-universal reaction of the "international community" to the current *intifida* and the succession of war crimes deployed to repress it continues to be to call for an end to violence (with the emphasis on *Palestinian* violence) and a return to negotiations. Negotiations about what? What will it take for the "international community" to recognize that the problem is not the resistance to the occupation but the occupation itself and that the goal must be to end the occupation, not to end the resistance?

The Palestinian people have made clear that they are prepared to pay a high price for their freedom, their dignity and their fundamental human rights. For most of them, the conditions of their lives are already so miserable and humiliating that the prospect of death with dignity is not an unattractive option. They have nothing left to lose. What will it take for the "international community" to start to live up to the

26

principles of international law and basic humanity which it professes to support – at least elsewhere?

One must always expect the worst from the United States and cannot be surprised that it would veto even sending unarmed observers to the occupied Palestinian territories. The United States would probably give unqualified support to Israel even if it pushed three million Palestinians, live, through a meatgrinder. However, one used to expect better from Europe. While obsessing daily over alleged war criminals in the former Yugoslavia, the European Union has greeted Ariel Sharon's assumption of power (and even the inclusion in his cabinet of Rehavam Zeevi, whose entire political career is founded on the advocacy of ethnically cleansing the entire indigenous population of historical Palestine) with apparent equanimity and has reacted to the ongoing and accelerating rape of Palestine with remarkable silence and passivity

It is particularly disappointing and depressing to see certain Arab governments adopting the Israeli-American analysis and priorities and publicly calling for an end to violence, rather than for an end to the occupation and solidarity with the Palestinian resistance.

The primordial requirement for peace must now be to make Ariel Sharon and all he represents appear, in Israeli eyes, even a worse disaster than Ehud Barak, so that the Israeli body politic undergoes a powerful laxative purge which produces a successor willing to get serious about actually achieving peace, not simply keeping a never-ending, so-called "peace process" twitching with faint signs of life, and which could cause Israeli public opinion to finally grasp the fundamental reality and essential truth that complying with international law and relevant UN resolutions and ending the occupation is profoundly in Israel's own self-interest.

Unfortunately, this will require that conditions on the ground get even worse in the short term in order for there to be any hope of their getting better in the long term. During the difficult months ahead, a far greater degree of Arab solidarity with the Palestinian people than has been demonstrated to date –

not simply on the rhetorical level but on the practical and financial levels – will be required. The Arab world has the means to summon the world's attention and to force it to take effective action on behalf of a genuine peace if its leaders can only summon the political will to do so.

Israelis love to recite, with a certain smugness, that "the Palestinians never miss an opportunity to miss an opportunity". If Israel had any true friends in the world, they would now be screaming that Israel is in the process of missing a golden opportunity that may never come again.

Since the 1991 Madrid Peace Conference, almost all Arab and Muslim states (including, most significantly, the State of Palestine) have been offering to accept the permanence of the Jewish State in the 78% of historical Palestine which the Zionist movement conquered in 1948 and which the "international community" has come to recognize as Israel's sovereign territory, even though this represents substantially more land than the UN proposed for the Jewish minority in its November 1947 partition resolution, in return for Israel's withdrawal to its internationally recognized borders in compliance with international law and relevant UN resolutions. This offer, if accepted, would have constituted an awesome achievement for the Zionist movement.

However, the Israelis wanted – and still want – more. Their spurning of this generous offer and their abuse of the "peace process" and of the goodwill of their Arab neighbors are changing the assumption of permanence in Arab eyes. The 78% offer may no longer be on the table – at least in the hearts and minds of most of the people of the Arab and Muslim states. It will certainly be off the table if Ariel Sharon's successor is not serious about actually achieving peace.

One thing should be clear to anyone with even a passing familiarity with the history of Palestine: Nothing is permanent except the presence of the Palestinian people. Historically, short-term interlopers have come and gone. The Crusader Kingdom in Palestine lasted for 88 years. So far, the Jewish State has lasted for 53 years. Unless a radical change in Israeli attitudes and direction occurs soon (and it is in everyone's interest that such a change *should* occur), a prudent person would hesitate to bet on the Jewish State's matching the 88-year lifespan of the Crusader Kingdom.

FEAR COULD BE THE KEY TO MIDDLE EAST PEACE

PUBLICATIONS:

October 2, 2001 – Jordan Times (Amman)
October 5 – Jerusalem Times
October 7 – Al-Quds (Jerusalem)
October 7 – Sunday Mail (Nicosia)
October 11 – Daily Star (Beirut)
October 14 – Arab News (Jeddah)
October 25 – Al-Ahram Weekly (Cairo)
November 2001 – Le Dossier Euro-Arabe (Paris)
December 2001 – Washington Report on Middle East Affairs

The hijacked aircraft which crashed in Pennsylvania on September 11 may well have had the U.S. Capitol, seat of the U.S. Congress, as its target. While we may never know for certain, if members of Congress suspect this to be true, their natural human response may provide the best hope in decades for actually achieving peace with some measure of justice in the Middle East.

It is widely believed that the same terrorist organization responsible for bringing down the World Trade Center was also behind the earlier bomb attack on it. It seems that the twin towers were "unfinished business". If the U.S. Congress views itself as "unfinished business" for terrorists who are filled with anti-American rage, determined, highly competent and suicidal (and who, if and when they try again, will almost certainly use a method not tried before and perhaps not even imagined yet), what is a rational member of Congress to do? Finally doing the right and decent thing in terms of U.S. Middle East policy should no longer be ruled out.

Foreign affairs experts outside the United States have long pounded their heads against walls trying to discern the American national interest served by the U.S. government's unconditional support for Israel's defiance of international law and UN resolutions through its continuing occupation of Arab lands conquered in 1967. This fruitless search for an explanation has been based on two false premises – that the United States has "national interests" (as opposed to simply the particular interests of particular special interest groups) and that American politicians genuinely care about "American national interests". Prior to September 11, when diminishing the risk of further massive terrorist attacks on American targets became a clear "national interest", there was little evidence to support either premise. America's Middle East policies have been based purely on the calculations of American politicians as to their personal self-interest.

American politicians are (with a few honorable exceptions) among the most selfish and self-interested people in one of the world's most selfish and self-interested countries. When it comes to Israel and Palestine, they are motivated overwhelmingly by fear – knee-knocking, sweaty-palmed, incontinent fear that the Israel-First Lobby will destroy their careers if they manifest anything less than total and abject subservience.

Roughly two decades ago, three prominent and highly respected members of Congress, Senators J. William Fulbright and Charles Percy and Representative Paul Findley, were perceived to have lost their seemingly "safe seats" due to massive Israel-First contributions to their electoral opponents. Their demise was particularly chilling since none of them had done anything that could be even remotely characterized as "anti-Israeli". They had simply supported balanced positions suggesting a willingness to put American interests ahead of Israeli desires. Ever since, American politicians have been paralyzed by the fear of being "Percyed" or "Findleyed".

The alternative explanation for the behavior of American politicians, that it is based on "conviction" (that is, that they support racism, apartheid and ethnic cleansing as a matter of principle), is clearly defamatory, attributing to them even a higher degree of moral and ethical bankruptcy than is justified.

31

After all, keeping one's job and advancing one's career is the principal focus of most people's lives, and no politician has ever lost an American election for being too supportive of Israel. So, what is a rational member of Congress, now with good reason to fear not just for his job and career but also for his life, to do? Surely a "repositioning" of the U.S. government's Middle East policy so as to make it consistent with international law, UN resolutions and the moral and ethical principles which America purports to support elsewhere could be accomplished without undue embarrassment.

Imagine that both houses of Congress adopted a resolution along the following lines: "This House believes that a just and durable peace in the Middle East can only be achieved on the basis of full compliance with international law and relevant UN resolutions by all states in the region. We believe that it is self-evident that Palestinian resistance to the Israeli occupation will continue as long as the occupation continues, that Israel will have peace and security when it ends the occupation but that Israel will never have either until it ends the occupation. The choice is Israel's to make, but we strongly urge Israel to choose peace and security by ending the occupation in all its aspects and withdrawing to its internationally recognized, pre-1967 borders."

If American politicians had ever cared genuinely about the best interests of Israel and Israelis, rather than simply about their own reelections, they would have said something similar long ago. While such a "repositioning" by the United States would be most unlikely to change the policies of the Sharon regime, it would be likely to accelerate its replacement by a new Israeli government with which a renewed peace process could actually produce peace, not simply more process.

It would also, in a moment, lift the sense of menace currently hanging over the United States and the world. Anti-American rage is not an incurable congenital disease. It is a relatively recent development directly related to what America does in and to the rest of the world.

Terrorists strike at moments when they believe that their

acts will receive the highest level of support in the constituencies which they seek to please. (In this regard, the timing of the September 11 attacks so soon after the extraordinary American performance at the Durban Conference Against Racism and Racial Discrimination was surely no accident.) If the United States were to reverse direction and start treating Palestinians (and Arabs generally) as human beings entitled to basic human rights, support for inflicting further punishment on the United States would become minimal. The white-hot hatred of the United States prevalent in the Arab and Muslim worlds would cool dramatically. The multi-faceted "war on terrorism" would have scored a major victory.

For decades, the United States has been an obstacle to Middle East peace, not an asset. (If it had not existed, it is difficult to believe that the occupation would be entering its 35th year.) It would, of course, be prefereable if American policy changed for the right reasons, not simply as a result of the spirit of self-interest (indeed, self-preservation) of its politicians.

However, fundamental change away from America's illegal and immoral foreign policy positions and behavior with respect to the Middle East is clearly in the American national interest, in the interests of all who live in the region (including Israelis, most of whom would, like white South Africans, find the quality of their lives enhanced by escaping from the role of oppressors and enforcers of injustice) and in the interests of peace and human understanding in the 21st century.

If such a change occurs, even for a tragically wrong reason, and, as a result, the world is able to pull back from the abyss, those who lost their lives in the atrocities of September 11 will not have died in vain and the world will be a safer and better place for all who live in it.

ISRAELI-PALESTINIAN PEACE MUST BE IMPOSED

PUBLICATIONS:

November 4, 2001 – Arab News (Jeddah)
November 4 – Sunday Mail (Nicosia)
November 6 – Asharq Al-Awsat (London)
November 6 – Daily Star (Beirut)
November 7 – Jordan Times (Amman)
November 8 – Al-Ahram Weekly (Cairo)
November 9 – Al-Quds (Jerusalem)
November 16 – Jerusalem Times
December 6 – The Independent (London)
December 7 – Middle East International (London)
January/February 2002 – Washington Report on Middle East Affairs

If all the established powers that be – the United States, the European Union, the Arab League, Israel and the Palestinian Authority – publicly profess to agree on anything, the subject of their agreement should be rigorously examined to determine whether it makes any sense. The conventional wisdom that Israeli-Palestinian violence should end and negotiations between the Israeli and Palestinian leaderships should resume makes no sense whatsoever – at least for Israelis and Palestinians.

It is, of course, unorthodox to appear to support violence (other than violence engaged in by the United States) or to oppose negotiations (other than negotiations with "terrorists"), but the intractability and critical importance of the Israeli-Palestinian conflict calls for unorthodox thinking.

Palestinians are being urged to renounce the internationally recognized right of resistance to an illegal occupation in return for the opportunity to negotiate with Ariel Sharon, who has just announced his intention to lead any negotiations personally. If anyone had suggested to the leaders and people of occupied Kuwait that they should renounce resistance and negotiate with Saddam Hussein, such a suggestion would have been branded, correctly, as absurd and immoral. The conventional wisdom of the "international community" that the Palestinians should renounce resistance and negotiate with Ariel Sharon is no less absurd and immoral. It is true that it is in the selfish interests of almost all established governments for the Israeli-Palestinian conflict to "go quiet" for a while. The daily televised death and destruction are inconvenient and bothersome for the international establishment, threatening the stability of certain regimes in the region and potentially interfering with other wars deemed, for the moment, more important.

However, it should be obvious that Arafat-Sharon negotiations, if they ever happened, would only provide a very brief lull in the hostilities before they flared up again, probably even more ferociously. The Israeli and Palestinian peoples desperately need to put a definitive end to their conflict. With the occupation in its 35th year, the time to do so is finally ripe, but it will never happen if Israelis and Palestinians are left to their own devices and the traditional American formulation that "whatever is acceptable to the parties is acceptable to us" (an elegant way of saying that law is irrelevant and "might makes right") remains the framework for any "peace process".

It is now exactly ten years since the current "peace process" began at the post-Gulf War Madrid Conference. It has, sadly, produced a great deal of "process" and no peace. If the current conventional wisdom continues to prevail, the world will no doubt be discussing how to revive the "peace process" ten years from now – indeed, probably 20 and 30 years from now. By definition, so long as there is a "peace process", there is no peace.

It should now be clear that the issues separating Israelis and Palestinians are too difficult and too emotionally charged for any Israeli leadership (let alone Ariel Sharon) and any Palestinian leadership (even Yasser Arafat) to reach a definitive peace agreement through bilateral negotiations. Indeed, on the Israeli side, this realization has already taken hold and led to much discussion of unilateralist "solutions" to be imposed by Israel on Palestine.

If negotiations are recognized to be pointless (except for producing temporary lulls in violence), what are the alternatives? The first alternative is a continuation of the status quo, with each side hoping to inflict so much pain on the other side over a sustained period of time that the other side eventually loses heart and gives them what they failed to achieve through negotiations – an end to the occupation or acquiescence in the occupation.

It is most unlikely that either side will obtain satisfaction of such hopes by such means in the foreseeable future. However, such a strategy does make somewhat more sense from a Palestinian perspective than from an Israeli one. While the chances of obtaining an end to the occupation through sustained violence are slim, the chances of obtaining an end to the occupation through bilateral negotiations alone are as non-existent as the chances of the Palestinians ever acquiescing in a permanent occupation, however restructured and relabeled.

The second alternative is for the "international community" to impose peace on the belligerents, leaving their respective leaderships no choice and thereby relieving them of the need to agree to anything (other than minor details of implementation) with the other side. To actually be implemented and to last, any peace must, of course, be perceived to be just and consistent with international law.

A special session of the UN General Assembly could be convened to put practical, up-to-date flesh on General Assembly Resolution 181 of November 1947, which recommended the partition of Palestine into two states. The fundamental parameters to be fixed would necessarily not be fully acceptable to either side but would be firmly rooted in international law and relevant UN resolutions and would not be subject to contestation or negotiation.

If the General Assembly acted wisely, these parameters would be consistent, in particular, with two fundamental principles of international law. First, the "inadmissibility of the acquisition of territory by war", an essential principle of the post-World War II world order which is emphasized in the first recital to Security Council Resolution 242. This would confirm as the borders of the two states the lines of control existing prior to the June 1967 war. Second, the sovereign right of every state to determine who has a right of residence in that state. This would mean that only those Israelis acceptable to Palestine would have a right of residence in Palestine and only those Palestinians acceptable to Israel would have a right of residence in Israel.

These principles are clear and comprehensible. Any variation from them or effort to "compromise" on them would lead away from a durable peace and back to the swamp of a never-ending "process". If all current Israeli settlements on Palestinian land occupied in 1967 were eventually evacuated but left intact and in good condition, then, particularly in light of the proven ability of Palestinians to live more tightly packed than Israelis, there might already be available sufficient (indeed, superior) housing for all Palestinian refugees currently outside historic Palestine who would prefer return to the State of Palestine to other alternatives for resettlement (which should be made simultaneously and generously available for their free choice), as well as for many currently living in refugee camps within historic Palestine.

The United States has no veto in the General Assembly, so its leverage to water down any resolution there so as to make it unjust and inconsistent with international law (and thus to ensure that it would not produce peace) would be limited. If a constructive and principled General Assembly resolution along the above lines were passed on to the Security Council, the body capable of transforming recommendations into binding international law, for its ratification, the United States would know that a veto would cost it all remaining regional support for its war against Afghanistan. This just might motivate the United States, if only for the wrong reason, to do the right thing.

Further Israeli-Palestinian negotiations are a dead end, not a viable option for peace. The only alternatives are

37

continuing violence and a just peace imposed on the parties to the conflict by the United Nations. The latter alternative is much the better one, and it is urgent.

"TERRORISM": THE WORD ITSELF IS DANGEROUS

PUBLICATIONS:

December 7, 2001 – Daily Star (Beirut)
December 9 – Asharq Al-Awsat (London)
December 10 – Jordan Times (Amman)
December 13 – Al-Ahram Weekly (Cairo)
December 14 – Al-Quds (Jerusalem)
December 17 – Arab News (Jeddah)
December 21 – Jerusalem Times
March 2002 – Washington Report on Middle East Affairs
March 10 – Los Angeles Times
March 15 – Cyprus Mail (Nicosia)
April 2002 – Arabies Trends (Paris)
April 7 – Gulf Times (Doha)
April 9 – Gulf News (Dubai)
May 28 – Dagbladet Arbejderen (Copenhagen)

The greatest threat to world peace today is clearly "terrorism" – not the behavior to which the word is applied but the word itself.

For years, people have recited the truisms that "One man's terrorist is another man's freedom fighter" and that "Terrorism, like beauty, is in the eye of the beholder". However, with the world's sole superpower declaring an open-ended, worldwide "war on terrorism", the notorious subjectivity of this word is no longer a joke.

It is no accident that there is no agreed definition of "terrorism", since the word is so subjective as to be devoid of any inherent meaning. At the same time, the word is extremely dangerous, because people tend to believe that it does have meaning and to use and abuse the word by applying it to whatever they hate as a way of avoiding rational thought and discussion and, frequently, excusing their own illegal and immoral behavior.

There is no shortage of precise verbal formulations for the diverse acts to which the word "terrorism" is often applied. "Mass murder", "assassination", "arson" and "sabotage" are available (to all of which the phrase "politically motivated" can be added if appropriate), and such crimes are already on the statute books, rendering specific criminal legislation for "terrorism" unnecessary. However, such precise formulations do not carry the overwhelming, demonizing and thought-deadening impact of the word "terrorism", which is, of course, precisely the charm of the word for its more cynical and unprincipled users and abusers. If someone commits "politically motivated mass murder", people might be curious as to the cause or grievances which inspired such a crime, but no cause or grievance can justify (or even explain) "terrorism", which, all right-thinking people agree, is the ultimate evil.

Most acts to which the word "terrorism" is applied (at least in the West) are tactics of the weak, usually (although not always) against the strong. Such acts are not a tactic of choice but of last resort. To cite one example, the Palestinians would certainly prefer to be able to fight for their freedom by "respectable" means, using F-16's, Apache attack helicopters and laser-guided missiles such as those the United States provides to Israel. If the United States provided such weapons to Palestine as well, the problem of suicide bombers would be solved. Until it does, or at least for so long as the Palestinians can see no hope for a decent future, no one should be surprised or shocked that Palestinians use the "delivery systems" available to them – their own bodies. Genuine hope for something better than a life worse than death is the only cure for the despair which inspires such gruesome violence.

In this regard, it is worth noting that the poor, the weak and the oppressed rarely complain about "terrorism". The rich, the strong and the oppressors constantly do. While most of mankind has more reason to fear the high-technology violence of the strong than the low-technology violence of the weak, the fundamental mind-trick employed by the abusers of the epithet "terrorism" (no doubt, in some cases, unconsciously) is essentially this: The low-technology violence of the weak is such an abomination that there are no limits on the high-technology violence of the strong which can be deployed against it.

Not surprisingly, since September 11, virtually every recognized state confronting an insurgency or separatist movement has eagerly jumped on the "war on terrorism" bandwagon, branding its domestic opponents (if it had not already done so) "terrorists" and, at least implicitly, taking the position that, since no one dares to criticize the United States for doing whatever it deems necessary in its "war on terrorism", no one should criticize whatever they now do to suppress their own "terrorists". Even while accepting that many people labeled "terrorists" are genuinely reprehensible, it should be recognized that neither respect for human rights nor the human condition are likely to be enhanced by this apparent carte blanche seized by the strong to crush the weak as they see fit.

Writing in the Washington Post on October 15, Post Deputy Editor Jackson Diehl cited two prominent examples of the abuse of the epithet "terrorism": "With their handshake in the Kremlin, Sharon and Putin exchanged a common falsehood about the wars their armies are fighting against rebels in Chechnya and the West Bank and Gaza. In both cases, the underlying conflict is about national self-determination: statehood for the Palestinians, self-rule for Chechnya. The world is inclined to believe that both causes are just.... Sharon and Putin both have tried to convince the world that all their opponents are terrorists, which implies that the solution need not involve political concessions but merely a vigorous counterterrorism campaign."

Perhaps the only honest and globally workable definition of "terrorism" is an explicitly subjective one – "violence which I don't support". Anyone who reads both the Western and Arab press cannot help noticing that the Western press routinely characterizes as "terrorism" virtually all Palestinian violence against Israelis (even against Israeli occupation forces within Palestine), while the Arab press routinely characterizes as "terrorism" virtually all Israeli violence against Palestinians. Only this formulation would accomodate both characterizations, as well as most others.

However, the word has been so devalued that even violence is no longer an essential prerequisite for its use. In recently announcing a multi-billion-dollar lawsuit against ten international tobacco companies, a Saudi Arabian lawyer told the press: "We will demand that tobacco firms be included on the lists of terrorists and those financing and sponsoring terrorism because of the large number of victims that smoking has claimed the world over."

If everyone recognized that the word "terrorism" is fundamentally an epithet and a term of abuse, with no intrinsic meaning, there would be no more reason to worry about the word now than prior to September 11. However, with the United States relying on the word to assert, apparently, an absolute right to attack any country it dislikes (for the most part, countries Israel dislikes) and with President Bush repeatedly menacing that "either you're with us or you're with the terrorists" (which effectively means, "either you make our enemies your enemies or you'll be our enemy – and you know what we do to our enemies"), many people around the world must feel a genuine sense of terror (dictionary definition: "a state of intense fear") as to where the United States is taking the rest of the world.

Meanwhile, in America itself, the Bush Administration appears to be feeding the U.S. Constitution and America's traditions of civil liberties, due process and the rule of law (the finest aspects of American life and the principal reasons why the country used to be admired abroad) into a shredder – mostly to domestic applause or acquiescence. Who would have imagined that 19 angry men armed only with knives could accomplish so much, provoking a response, beyond their wildest dreams, which threatens to be vastly more damaging to their enemies even than their own appalling acts?

If the world is to avoid a descent into anarchy, in which the only rule is "might makes right", every "retaliation" provokes a "counter-retaliation" and a genuine "war of civilizations" is ignited, the world – and particularly the United States – must recognize that "terrorism" is simply a word, a subjective epithet, not an objective reality and certainly not an excuse to suspend all the rules of international law and domestic civil liberties which have, until now, made at least some parts of our planet decent places to live.

UN MEMBERSHIP FOR PALESTINE – NOW

PUBLICATIONS:

April 13, 2002 – Daily Star (Beirut)
April 14 – Arab News (Jeddah)
April 14 – Gulf Times (Doha)
April 16 – Al-Quds (Jerusalem)
April 18 – Al-Ahram Weekly (Cairo)
April 18 – Jordan Times (Amman)
April 19 – Asharq Al-Awsat (London)
April 19 – Jerusalem Times
May 19 – Gulf News (Dubai)
June 2002 – Arabies Trends (Paris)
June/July 2002 – Washington Report on Middle East Affairs

Note: This article was written during Israel's brutal spring 2002 invasion and re-occupation of the West Bank, which was then causing widespread deaths and destruction (particularly in Hebron and Jenin), including the destruction of Palestinian Authority offices and records. At this time, world (and even American) opinion was shocked by Israel's flagrant violations of Israeli–Palestinian agreements and its weeks–long pursuit of its offensive in defiance of worldwide appeals for restraint.

Counterintuitive though it may seem, now may be the ideal time for Palestine to apply for – and obtain – full United Nations membership. Indeed, UN membership for Palestine now would be the most constructive achievable response of the international community to Ariel Sharon's efforts to extinguish any Palestinian hope for eventual liberation from perpetual occupation, to the Likud Party Central Committee's vote against there ever being a Palestinian state "west of the Jordan River" and to Israel's blatant defiance of successive Security Council resolutions.

The State of Palestine was proclaimed, within all the Palestinian territories occupied during the 1967 war, on November 15, 1988 at the historic Palestine National Council meeting in Algiers which formally endorsed the two-state solution and recognized Israel within the 78% of historical Palestine which Israel had controlled prior to the 1967 war. Within two months, the State of Palestine was recognized diplomatically by over 100 other sovereign states. Today, it is recognized by roughly two-thirds of UN member states. Notwithstanding the subsequent Oslo accords, the state has never been renounced or legally ceased to exist. Indeed, in July 1998, by a 124-4 vote in the General Assembly, the "permanent observer" status of "Palestine" at the UN was upgraded to a unique and unprecedented level, with rights and privileges of participation that had previously been exclusive to member states.

The Palestinian Authority, an anomalous creature of the Oslo accords, legally ceased to exist on May 4, 1999, the date on which the "interim period" pursuant to these accords ended. No one having an interest in insisting upon this legal point, no one did. However, after Ariel Sharon's spring onslaught, the "Authority" has effectively ceased to exist as a practical force on the ground as well as in legal theory. The State of Palestine, which does not require a second proclaiming, is available to fill the vacuum.

After his return to Palestine in 1994, Yasser Arafat listed three titles under his signature on his Arabic correspondence – President of the State of Palestine, Chairman of the Executive Committee of the Palestine Liberation Organization and President of the "Palestinian National Authority". However, the state was de-emphasized and, publicly, spoken of more as an aspiration than as the legal and diplomatic fact which it actually was.

There were two good strategic reasons for this. First, the Palestinian leadership believed that discretion and peaceful negotiations were more likely to produce a warm and open peace based on the two-state solution than thrusting the Palestinian state aggressively in the face of an Israeli state which, after all, still occupied militarily all of Palestine. Second, the Palestinian leadership believed that, at each point when

45

bringing the state out of the closet was a serious prospect (indeed, on several occasions when President Arafat had solemnly promised to do so), a U.S. veto of UN membership was highly likely and might make the Palestinian position worse than before.

Neither of these concerns is valid today. A warm and open peace is no longer conceivable. It is now almost universally accepted that separation based on the two-state solution and on the pre-June 1967 borders is essential for the peace and security of both peoples. When, in late March, the Arab League dramatically reaffirmed this fundamental formula in its Beirut Declaration, inspired by the Saudi Arabian initiative, almost all governments publicly embraced it and not even Israel or the United States dared to publicly dismiss it.

In light of the events of recent days, who would dare to oppose Palestine's admission to full UN membership if it were to apply now? The U.S. has, very belatedly, become aware of the white-hot anti-American rage boiling throughout the Arab and Muslim worlds. Demonstrators have attacked the American embassy in Bahrain, and other American embassies in the region have been spared attack only by vigorous police action.

At this point, particularly after President Bush has spoken repeatedly of his "vision" of a Palestinian state, would the U.S. dare to veto Palestine's UN membership? Perhaps for the first time ever, but during a window of opportunity which may not be open for long, an American veto is almost inconceivable.

If Palestine, within its internationally accepted pre-June 1967 borders, were a UN member state, not simply "the occupied territories" and no longer even arguably "disputed", for how much longer could Israel maintain its occupation, which even Kofi Annan now publicly brands "illegal"? The writing would clearly be on the wall for all to see. The end of the occupation, even if not imminent, would instantly become only a question of "when", no longer of "whether". No change currently imaginable is more likely than a mutual realization of this inevitability to reverse the accelerating cycle of violence.

It is now widely believed among Palestinians that the only conceivable way to end the occupation is to convince a majority of Israelis that it is in their personal self-interest to do so and that the only conceivable way to accomplish this is to kill Israelis in Israel – for as long as it takes. Western insistence that the Palestinians renounce violent resistance in return for the opportunity to negotiate with Ariel Sharon is viewed as a cruel joke.

A credible alternative to this brutal logic, capable of inspiring hope that the future may offer something better than a life worse than death, is desperately needed. UN membership and worldwide recognition of the State of Palestine – particularly if it were conferred in these darkest days of the occupation – could provide that alternative and that hope. It is an opportunity which can and must be seized.

INTERNATIONAL JUSTICE FOR ISRAEL AND PALESTINE

PUBLICATIONS:

June 30, 2002 – Sunday Mail (Nicosia)
July 3 – Arab News (Jeddah)
July 6 – Daily Star (Beirut)
July 7 – Asharq Al-Awsat (London)
July 7 – Jordan Times (Amman)
July 11 – Al-Ahram Weekly (Cairo)
July 12 – Jerusalem Times
August 2002 – Washington Report on Middle East Affairs
August 26 – Al-Quds (Jerusalem)

Late June was a brutal time for all who still hope for peace and justice in the Middle East – and not simply with respect to the violence, death and destruction on the ground.

On June 24, President George W. Bush delivered a hope-destroying speech on his "vision" for Middle East peace which combined overwhelming pro-Israeli bias with breathtaking logical absurdity and incoherence. (Writing in *The Guardian*, Jonathan Freedland called it a "fantastic speech" in the sense that it "consisted, from beginning to end, of fantasy.") This speech, which the world had been counting on to restore hope, virtually guarantees deepening despair and an acceleration of the already appalling violence, death and destruction. It is now clear that any progress toward peace must await regime change in the United States as well as in Israel.

Two days later, a Belgian court dismissed the complaint against Ariel Sharon for crimes against humanity arising out of his role in the Sabra and Shatilla massacres on the purely procedural (and, no doubt, politically pressured) grounds that Belgium's "universal jurisdiction" with respect to crimes against humanity only extends to persons physically present in Belgium.

What can seekers of peace and justice now do – if not to

48

improve the situation, at least to limit its deterioration? International law and the moral conscience of mankind have always been the Palestinians' only assets. These assets may be currently overwhelmed by the dominant principle of the new imperial order, "Might Makes Right", but there is now an opportunity to build on them which can and should be taken.

Having surpassed the required 60 ratifications in April, the Treaty of Rome establishing the International Criminal Court came into force on July 1. The court will have jurisdiction over those committing war crimes (notably including settlement activity) and crimes against humanity after July 1. There are, of course, various exceptions and exclusions, many insisted upon by the United States as a condition to its signing the treaty. (In the end, the United States and Israel were among the seven states, out of 127, participating in the Rome Conference not to sign the treaty at the conclusion of the conference – perhaps, at least in part, due to their failure to obtain an exclusion for settlement activity.)

One exclusion successfully negotiated by the United States is highly relevant to the Middle East. For the court to have jurisdiction, either the alleged criminal must come from a ratifying state or the alleged crime must be committed in a ratifying state. Since Israel is most unlikely ever to ratify the treaty and since Palestine is not (at least yet) a ratifying state, this carefully crafted legal loophole means that Israelis can continue to commit war crimes and crimes against humanity in the occupied Palestinian territories with no fear that their crimes might lead to their being brought to justice in The Hague.

However, what is to prevent the State of Palestine, which was proclaimed in 1988 and has been recognized diplomatically by more than 120 other sovereign states, from signing and ratifying the treaty and presenting its instrument of ratification to the United Nations, where, although Palestine has not applied for full member state status, it enjoys permanent observer status with most of the rights of a member state?

While the United States can veto full United Nations membership for Palestine, it cannot veto a state's accession to an international treaty to which the United States is not itself a party. It might try to twist Secretary General Kofi Annan's arm to fend off Palestine's instrument of ratification, but on what basis?

President Bush could scarcely have been more vigorous or insistent that the Palestinian leadership must "do more" to fight "terrorism". If Palestine were a ratifying state of the Treaty of Rome, then any Palestinian, at any level, committing a "terrorist" act which constitutes a war crime or a crime against humanity could be brought to justice before the International Criminal Court, which would not be the case in the absence of Palestinian ratification.

How could the United States oppose this? More precisely, how could it explain its opposition? Because making Palestinians subject to international criminal law would, indirectly, make Israelis committing war crimes and crimes against humanity in the occupied Palestinian territories also subject to international criminal law? Because the United States prefers targeted assassinations and extrajudicial executions to the rule of law?

Not incidentally, Palestinian accession to the Treaty of Rome would entail official United Nations recognition of Palestine as a "state", existing today, with nothing "provisional" about it. At least as importantly, every Israeli politician, every Israeli soldier and every Israeli settler would then know that "business as usual" would put them at some risk (however modest) of indictment, of arrest in other countries and of being tried before the International Criminal Court. This knowledge could have some restraining effect on the behavior of some of them.

This recourse to international law would not overrule the principle that "Might Makes Right". However, it could moderate and reduce somewhat the intensity of the violence, death and destruction which both Palestinians and Israelis will have to suffer while waiting for the Palestinian leadership (any Palestinian leadership) to have true partners for peace in the Israeli and American leaderships. It could be a long wait.

50

Moderating the brutality, saving lives and strengthening the rule of law against the law of the jungle are well worth the effort.

"MASTER-BLASTER" – A CASE FOR LIBERATION

PUBLICATIONS:

April 26, 2003 – Arab News (Jeddah)
May 1 – Al-Quds (Jerusalem)
May 2 – Daily Star (Beirut)
May 2 – Jerusalem Times
May 3 – Asharq Al-Awsat (London)
May 8 – Jordan Times (Amman)
May 11 – Sunday Mail (Nicosia)
May 15 – Al-Ahram Weekly (Cairo)
June 2003 – Washington Report on Middle East Affairs

In the film "Thunderdome", part of the bleak and violent "Mad Max" series of films, there were two memorable characters – sultry pop diva Tina Turner and "Master-Blaster". In the film's post-nuclear-war wasteland without petroleum, the only source of energy was pig excrement, produced and processed in a grim underworld ruled over by Master-Blaster, a composite, two-in-one character. "Blaster" was a huge, muscle-bound adolescent with (to be polite) severely underdeveloped mental abilities. On his shoulders, hidden under a large helmet, sat "Master", a brilliant midget who did Master-Blaster's thinking and provided the character's voice while harnessing Blaster's brute force to achieve wildly disproportionate power for a midget.

Master-Blaster is an extraordinarily apt personification of the bizarre relationship between Israel and the United States in recent decades. This is particularly the case under the current Sharon-Bush regime. Encouragingly, even the "mainstream" press in the United States has started, albeit hesitantly and delicately, to focus on who is doing the thinking behind current American foreign policy and (in the case of a few brave voices) for whose benefit they are doing this thinking.

As Anne Joyce, Editor of the Washington quarterly *Middle East Policy*, has courageously written in the current issue of this journal, the war on Iraq was "planned, not to protect the American homeland from the weak Saddam Hussein, but to consolidate an American hegemony in the Middle East that will permit Israeli settlers to keep the land they are stealing from the Palestinians."

A key question which needs to be posed more widely and intensely is in what respects (if any) a series of American wars against Israel's enemies (let alone the perpetual "full-spectrum domination" of the entire world by the Israeli-American Empire so dear to the hearts and minds of the "neoconservative" cabal doing the thinking behind current American foreign policy) is likely (or even intended) to improve the security, prosperity or quality of life of *Americans*. It is a question for which honest and convincing answers are not obvious.

Those who defend the regime's "neoconservatives" against suggestions of "dual loyalties" (a rather generous verbal formulation in the circumstances) often argue that, in fact, they make no distinction in their own minds between the United States and Israel, genuinely viewing the interests of the two countries as identical in all circumstances and honestly considering whatever is good for Israel to be good for the United States. This may well be an accurate reflection of the state of mind of many "neoconservatives" – and, indeed, for reasons of conviction or fear, of the editorial policy of most of the American media. However, many Americans, particularly those who, post-September 11, do not accept "because we love freedom" as an honest and convincing answer to the question "Why do they hate us?", do not view Master-Blaster as a single character on the world stage.

It requires great courage for anyone in the United States to question publicly this alleged identity of national interests. (The members of the U.S. Congress who would dare to state publicly that Israeli and American interests are not always identical and that they would always put American interests ahead of Israeli interests could probably be counted on one person's fingers.) Anyone challenging the prevailing orthodoxy in an effective manner can expect to be hit with the epithet of mass destruction "anti-Semite", which, in America, is more intimidating than "anti-American". This does not make challenges less essential for those who genuinely care about American national interests or world peace.

Master seems to be getting so certain of his dominant position wrapped around Blaster's head that he no longer even exercises due care in hiding himself under the helmet. Ariel Sharon has been famously quoted as telling Shimon Peres, while the latter was serving as his fig-leaf foreign minister, that Israel had no reason to worry about American "pressure", because "Israel controls the United States." Promptly after the fall of Baghdad, an interview in the Tel Aviv daily newspaper *Ma'ariv* quoted Israeli defense minister Shaul Mofaz as saying, "We have a long line of issues we are thinking of demanding of the Syrians, and it would best be done through the Americans" – who, of course, promptly did so.

Perhaps, at some point, the "liberation" of Iraq from Iraqi rule (and of Syria from Syrian rule?) will be followed by the liberation of the United States from foreign domination. In the film's revolutionary climax, Master is knocked off Blaster's shoulders and drowns in a vat of liquefied power, while Blaster, suddenly his own man, finds his voice and, finally, speaks for himself.

A HERETICAL THOUGHT FOR PEACE

PUBLICATIONS:

June 12, 2003 – Al-Ahram Weekly (Cairo)
June 12 – Al-Quds (Jerusalem)
June 13 – Jerusalem Times
June 14 – Arab News (Jeddah)
June 16 – Daily Star (Beirut)
June 16 – Jordan Times (Amman)
June 21 – Asharq Al-Awsat (London)
June 22 – Sunday Mail (Nicosia)
July/Aug. 2003 – Washington Report on Middle East Affairs
October 1 – International Herald Tribune (Paris)
October 4 – Al-Mustaqbal (Beirut)
October 5 – Gulf Times (Doha)
October 26 – Al-Eqtisadiah (Jeddah)

In early June, the respected Pew Research Center in the United States released the latest of its global opinion surveys, which polled more than 15,000 people in 21 countries in the wake of the invasion and conquest of Iraq. The results attracted considerable attention in the American press.

A primary focus of press reports was the surge of anti-American sentiment in the Muslim world. In traditionally pro-American Jordan, 97% of those polled opposed America's "war on terror", while, in NATO-member Turkey, 83% expressed an unfavorable opinion of the United States. The selection of Osama bin Laden by the publics of five of the eight Muslim countries surveyed (Indonesia, Jordan, Morocco, Pakistan and Palestine) as one of the three political leaders they would most trust to "do the right thing" in world affairs did not go unnoticed.

Less noticed, but no less significant, were the responses to another question. Those polled were asked whether the United States is too supportive of Israel. In 20 of the 21 countries surveyed (notably *including* Israel), most of those polled said "yes". There is no prize for guessing the one country where most said "no".

Israeli support for this proposition should not come as a complete surprise. Israelis have to live in Israel/Palestine. While their lives since Ariel Sharon provoked the current intifada in September 2000 have not been the living hell experienced by Palestinians, they have still become unpleasant, insecure and stressful. Increasingly, the essential realization that occupation and security are mutually exclusive has been sinking in.

No American national interest is served by Israel's continuing occupation of the Arab lands which it conquered in 1967. American supporters of the occupation tend to be Christian fundamentalists concerned about being personally raptured up to heaven after the much-to-be-hoped-for Battle of Armageddon, Jews who feel personally guilty to be living prosperously and comfortably in America rather than having emigrated to Israel/Palestine or politicians interested only in preserving or furthering their personal careers by not offending the other two groups.

Americans in these three groups, which are critical to the formulation of American Middle East policy, do not have to suffer the consequences of the occupation or the resistance to it, and their support for the occupation rarely reflects any genuine concern for the best interests of Israelis (let alone Palestininians). Their militant "pro-Israel" activism is purely self-centered and selfish in its motivation. It is also the primary obstacle to peace.

Those Israelis who feel that America is too supportive of Israel presumably can see that America's involvement since 1967 has not advanced the cause of peace but, rather, has blocked it, with America's periodic pretenses of peacemaking simply providing an "only game in town" cover behind which the occupation could be perpetuated, deepened and made more nearly irreversible. They presumably wish, for their own sakes, that America would "reform".

Now – a heretical thought. Virtually all governments and commentators agree, at least in their public pronouncements, that deeper engagement by the United States is essential if Israeli-Palestinian peace is ever to be achieved. Wrong. The best hope for peace would be total American disengagement – and the sooner the better.

Imagine that the U.S. Government were to announce that it was washing its hands of the Israeli-Palestinian conflict, that it would no longer give any military, economic or diplomatic aid or support to either side and that it would not use its veto to block any UN Security Council resolution with respect to Israel/Palestine, even one imposing sanctions on either or both of the parties to the conflict. Having never been an "honest broker", the United States would at least become an honest bystander.

Israeli politicians and American Christian fundamentalists would be appalled. However, if the Pew poll is to be believed, many Israelis would be relieved – and finally see light at the end of the tunnel. With the the U.S. out of the picture, the occupation would become, and be recognized to be, unsustainable. The great boulder blocking the road to peace would have rolled itself out of the way, and the road to peace (not to be confused with the "road map") could finally be open for travel.

As a hugely beneficial side-effect, American disengagement would, with immediate effect, vastly diminish anti-American rage throughout the Muslim world and the consequent threat of further "terrorist" attacks on Americans and American interests. There would no longer be any need to continue the series of wars against Israel's (hence America's) enemies. American civil liberties could be restored, and hundreds of billions of dollars could be redirected in constructive ways that would actually enhance the quality of life of Americans. The United States might even become respected out of admiration, as it once was, rather than simply out of fear, as it now is.

A dream? Of course. Just a dream. America will continue to block the road to peace, and America – and the world – will continue to pay a massive price for this.

MIDDLE EAST SURPRISES FOR AMERICA

PUBLICATIONS:

July 10, 2003 – Arab News (Jeddah)
July 13 – Asharq Al-Awsat (London)
July 14 – Jordan Times (Amman)
July 17 – Al-Ahram Weekly (Cairo)
July 17 – Al-Quds (Jerusalem)
July 18 – Jerusalem Times
July 20 – Sunday Mail (Nicosia)
July 25 – International Herald Tribune (Paris)
September 2003 – Washington Report on Middle East Affairs
Fall 2003 – GOAB-Bulletin (Vienna)

For those formulating American foreign policy and dreaming of remaking the Middle East in their own image, the region appears to be full of surprises. The determined resistance of some Iraqis to the Western occupation of their country seems to have been genuinely unanticipated. It should not have been. If the United States were conquered and occupied by Arab armies which announced their intention to stay for years and to restructure the country's government and economy along Islamic lines, would not Americans – and not just "hardcore Bush loyalists" or "Republican Party remnants" – resist?

The legislative elections in Kuwait on July 5, if noticed in America, should have constituted an even more stunning surprise. Before and after the conquest of Iraq, proponents of the war evoked the vision of a virtuous "domino effect" toppling authoritarian regimes in the region and replacing them with modernizing, Western-oriented "democratic" ones. As a genuine reason for war, such a democratic mission always lacked credibility with those who actually live in the region, who recognize that, so long as America and Israel act like Siamese twins joined at the brain, any government in the Arab world which actually reflected the will of its people would be fervently anti-American.

Of course, Americans do like elections – provided that they produce the "right" result. (Donald Rumsfeld has made clear that an Islamic government will not be permitted in Iraq even if most of Iraq's people were to favor one.) However, few believe that the United States would really prefer a democratically elected government which is anti-American to an authoritarian regime which is pro-American.

So, what happened in the elections in Kuwait, the most pro-American country in the Arab world, with the most reason (by far) to be pro-American? The "liberals", who seek a more open and modern society and had hoped to make significant gains, were almost wiped out, retaining only three seats (down from eight) in the 50-seat parliament. The remaining 47 seats went to conservatives and Islamists, including radical fundamentalists. The "domino effect" has not worked out – at least not falling in the "right" direction – next door to Iraq. What would genuinely fair elections produce in other Arab countries, whose people are far less pro-American? A quiet burial for the "democratic mission" can be anticipated.

Another illusion destined to be dispelled soon is that the current "road map" for Israel/Palestine will win the United States friends and gratitude in the Arab world, diminishing the anger aroused by the conquest and occupation of Iraq. While the "road map" is widely described as a "peace plan", in Arab eyes, "peace" in Israel/Palestine requires ending the occupation, not crushing all resistance to it, while, in most of the world, true "peace" is recognized to require some measure of "justice", a word rigorously avoided by successive American governments in connection with their successive "peace plans".

If one reads the "road map", it is readily apparent that it builds on a false premise to reach an unbelievable conclusion. The premise is that the problem in Israel/Palestine is Palestinian resistance to the 36-year-long occupation, not the occupation itself. The conclusion is that, *if* the Palestinian leadership will first suppress completely all forms of resistance to the occupation and eliminate all capabilities for ever resisting again, thereby making the occupation totally cost-free for Israelis, *then* (and only then) Israel will choose, of its own free will, to end the occupation, withdrawing to (essentially) its internationally recognized pre-1967 borders, vacating the settlements, sharing Jerusalem and agreeing to a just settlement of the refugee issue.

The Holy Land may, in theory, be a land of miracles, but, even if the "*if*" were possible at the start of the road (which is most unlikely), it is difficult to believe that anyone in a state of sobriety could genuinely believe that the "*then*" would follow. (By contrast, if such a destination, fully consistent with international law, were announced and guaranteed at the start of the road, as it would be in any peace plan devised with a sincere intention to achieve peace, there would no longer be any need for resistance.)

Arabs are not fools. Even if they have not read the "road map", when they see both George W. Bush and Colin Powell insisting that a total cessation of Palestinian violence is not good enough and that the Palestinian leadership must also eliminate any capability for resuming violent resistance in the future, they can recognize that the true American objective is not "peace", as they understand the word, but, at best, simply "quiet" – Palestinian acquiescence in the occupation and acceptance of whatever terms Israel may wish to impose on a defeated and demoralized people – and, at worst, provoking a Palestinian civil war.

Such a "peace plan" will win the United States no more friends and gratitude in the Arab world than American efforts to repress resistance to its own occupation of a proud Arab country by ever-escalating force, which is condemned to produce ever-intensifying resistance, which will be met by yet more brutal force in an infernal cycle which Israelis and Palestinians know all too well.

Is there any way to prevent an already ugly situation in the Middle East from degenerating into a long-term war of civilizations? Actually, there is. In March 2002, the Arab League, in its Beirut Declaration, dramatically offered full peace and normal diplomatic and economic relations between Israel and all Arab states in return for a total end to the occupation of all Arab lands occupied in 1967. The Arab League should formally reaffirm this offer, while also making clear the "other side of the coin" – that there will never be peace or normal relations until the occupation ends.

Then, the United States should make clear that what must end – and soon – is the occupation, not the resistance to it. Of course, for America to do so would require a virtual "second American declaration of independence". American politicians would have to put the interests of their own country and people ahead of the desires of extreme right-wing elements in Israel and their vocal, intimidating and well-funded supporters in the United States. Most observers would consider such a revolution inconceivable, but, at least in theory, it is possible – and it is urgent.

The true "road map" confronting Iraq, Palestine and the region as a whole is not one of steady progress toward peace, prosperity, Western-style democracy and increasingly pro-American sentiments. Unless the world focuses soon on the real problem and its only real solution, and insists on the prompt implementation of that solution, we are all risking a rapid descent into hell.

THE ARAB WORLD IS NOT IMPOTENT

PUBLICATIONS:

October 11, 2003 – Arab News (Jeddah)
October 13 – Al-Quds (Jerusalem)
October 14 – Jordan Times (Amman)
October 16 – Al-Ahram Weekly (Cairo)
October 17 – Jerusalem Times
October 18 – Asharq Al-Awsat (London)

The feebleness, even on a rhetorical level, of the official Arab response to Israel's bombing raid deep inside Syrian territory has given rise to renewed lamentations regarding the humiliating impotence of the Arab world. As an editorial in the *Arab News* (Jeddah) has stated, "Impotence is a strong word, but impotence is precisely what Arabs on the street feel." However, the impotence so widely perceived and felt is not an objective fatality. It is a political choice.

While its leaders may not realize it, the Arab world is not impotent. Indeed, it has it within its power to achieve peace with some measure of justice – not in some distant future but soon and not through enhanced violence but through the intelligent and responsible application of restrained but sustained economic pressure.

A concerted, concrete and effective plan of action could take the form of a simple, easily understood and ethically unimpeachable "carrot-and-stick" approach, with both "carrot" and "stick" announced simultaneously.

First, the "carrot": The Arab League would formally reaffirm the wise and generous peace terms contained in its Beirut Declaration of March 2002, inspired by Crown Prince Abdullah's courageous initiative, which offered full peace and normal diplomatic and economic relations between Israel and all Arab states in return for a total end to the occupation of all Arab lands occupied by Israel in 1967. Some doubt that this offer, which was clearly the most generous one Israel will ever receive, is still on the table. The Arab states should make clear that, at least for the time being, it is – and they should mean it.

Second, the "stick": The major Arab and Muslim oil producers would state that, until Israel complies fully with international law and UN resolutions by withdrawing from *all* occupied Arab land to its internationally recognized borders, they will reduce their petroleum exports by increments of five percent each month – month after month after month – and they should mean it .

It would, of course, be preferable if the United States, whose unconditional support of Israel has made possible its continuing occupation of Arab lands and prevented the achievement of peace, were to undergo a moral and ethical transformation and if Americans were suddenly to realize both that Palestinians are human beings entitled to basic human rights and that international law should be complied with by all, not only by the poor, the weak and the Arab. Realistically, after so many years of antithetical attitudes, such a transformation is most unlikely to occur.

However, if Americans cannot be reached through their hearts or minds, they can be reached through their wallets. Money is the true religion of the United States. If oil prices were to soar and stock market prices were to plunge, Americans would be certain to start asking why, precisely, Israel *should* be permitted to continue defying international law and UN resolutions and denying Palestinians their basic human rights and why the United States, alone, should be unconditionally supporting it in doing so – at the cost of both worldwide anti-American rage and sharply higher oil prices for Americans.

Since no American national interests are served by Israel's continuing occupation of Arab lands, no credible, non-racist answers could be offered, and, with oil prices rising, stock market prices falling and no reversal of these trends in sight, these questions would become more insistent and Israel's defiant position could rapidly become untenable.

Under pressure even from their only unconditional supporters, Israelis might well recognize, sooner than anyone would dare to hope today, that their own security will never be ensured so long as they illegally occupy any Arab lands and that full compliance with international law and UN resolutions, in Palestine and Syria just as in Egypt, Jordan and Lebanon, is profoundly in Israel's own long-term self-interest, has in any event become unavoidable and should therefore be embraced sooner rather than later.

While waiting for economic discomfort to stimulate common sense and produce the result that serves the interests of all, Arab and Muslim petroleum producers would suffer no pain or sacrifices. Each five percent reduction in exports should result in a greater than five percent increase in prices, and moderate but regular reductions in exports, unlike a sudden total embargo, should be technically, politically and psychologically sustainable.

Does no one in the Arab world recall the courageous leadership of King Faisal 30 years ago this month? For a brief, shining moment, the Arab world was respected. "Respect" is not a word anyone would associate with the Arab world today. Rather, as Western occupation armies rule Iraq and high figures in the Bush administration talk publicly of redrawing the map of the region to better serve Israeli and American interests, the Arab world's status approaches that of Africa when the imperial powers gathered at the Berlin Conference of 1885 to carve the continent up among themselves.

There is nothing inevitable about this. Impotence is not an unavoidable fact, and despair and resignation are not the only options. The source of the strength which King Faisal wielded so effectively is still there. All that is needed is the courage and leadership to use it wisely.

THE GENEVA ACCORD: THE REAL ROAD TO PEACE

PUBLICATIONS:

November 30, 2003 – Al-Quds (Jerusalem)
December 1 – Arab News (Jeddah)
December 1 – Jordan Times (Amman)
December 3 – Gulf Times (Doha)
December 4 – Al-Ahram Weekly (Cairo)
December 5 – Asharq Al-Awsat (London)
December 5 – Financial Times (London)
December 12 – Jerusalem Times
December 13 – Daily Star (Beirut)
December 14 – Sunday Mail (Nicosia)
January/February 2004 – Washington Report on Middle East Affairs
January 8, 2004 – Al-Ahram Weekly (expanded version)

The "Geneva Accord", signed on December 1 at an impressive ceremony in which President Jimmy Carter and other Nobel Peace Prize laureates participated, deserves the active and whole-hearted support of everyone who genuinely cares about Israelis, Palestinians or peace.

This "virtual" permanent-status peace agreement is a prodigious, detailed document containing all the fundamental substantive compromises and trade-offs which have long been recognized to be necessary in any negotiated peace agreement which could conceivably be acceptable both to most Israelis and to most Palestinians, as well as carefully considered procedures and timelines for implementation. If both peoples simultaneously had governments which were sincerely determined to achieve peace, this is precisely the sort of document one would expect to emerge from their negotiations. It is not simply "symbolic". As Yasser Abed Rabbo said in Geneva, "it is the only possible solution".

Naturally, neither side would realize all of its dreams

65

under the Geneva Accord. It would not implement all of the Palestinians' rights under international law, notably with respect to the right of return for refugees. However, Palestinians should recognize that, if they were to reject peace on this basis, it would be vastly more likely that the Zionist project would be carried through to its logical conclusion – the total ethnic cleansing of the entire indigenous population of Palestine – than that they would ever achieve all of their rights under international law through negotiations.

Israelis would have to settle for 78 percent of historic Palestine, relinquish the dream of carrying the Zionist project through to its logical conclusion and accept Palestinians as human beings entitled to basic human rights and their permanent neighbors, but they would not have to relinquish any of their rights under international law. Israelis should recognize that, if they were to reject peace on this basis, they would be opting for an open-ended fight to the finish between a few million Israeli Jews and over a billion Muslims. Any true friends of Israel, Israelis and the Jewish people should shout out loudly and clearly that, in any long-term perspective, this would be a catastrophically bad choice.

Efforts to achieve peace through bilateral negotiations between Israeli and Palestinian governments have failed, and there is scant reason to hope that they will ever succeed. Appeals to the United States or the United Nations to impose a solution on the parties will, for reasons of American domestic politics, remain unanswered.

The Geneva Accord offers another, more promising way forward. First, prominent peace-oriented Israeli and Palestinian politicians, while temporarily out of government, negotiate and sign a comprehensive and implementable peace agreement. Then they appeal to the Israeli and Palestinian peoples to bring to power governments that will implement the peace agreement already reached.

The hope, verging on a likelihood, is that, if a potential coalition of Israeli political parties were, in an election campaign, to offer the Israeli electorate a completed, pre-agreed peace agreement with terms close to the best that Israelis could rationally hope for and a clear choice between a prompt and permanent peace on those terms or more of the same (or worse), a majority of Israelis would choose peace.

Israel is not legally obligated to hold new elections for several years. However, early elections have been the rule rather than the exception in Israel, where governments often fall for reasons that seem trivial or barely comprehensible to outsiders. Yitzhak Rabin's first term as prime minister ended because his wife had left a few thousand dollars in a Washington bank account after his tour as ambassador there. Ariel Sharon is currently being investigated for financial crimes on a grander scale. Settlements are a potential minefield within the current coalition. The next Israeli elections may not, in fact, be years away, and the Geneva Accord, if widely supported, might bring them closer.

Even those who believe that the "road map" was conceived with good intentions should by now recognize that it was misconceived, leads nowhere and should be set aside. Why should anyone who genuinely seeks peace insist on spending further years wandering through a heavily mined labyrinth toward an unidentified destination when the only possible peaceful destination has at last been identified and can now be approached directly?

The Geneva Accord has addressed and settled sensibly all the most difficult issues – Jerusalem, refugees, settlements and borders – which prior "peace plans" (including the "road map") postponed to a distant future unlikely ever to be reached. It must replace the "road map" as "the only game in town". Delay in implementing it will not improve the choices but only add to the toll of death and destruction – and not only in Israel and Palestine, since the absence of a decent and honorable Israeli-Palestinian peace is the principal catalyst of the current trends toward increased violence and terrorism and spiraling anti-American and anti-Israeli sentiment throughout the world.

At the signature ceremony, Yossi Beilin, the chief Israeli architect of the Geneva Accord, warned, "The opportunity to have pragmatic partners belonging to the mainstream of our two societies is not open-ended. If the right steps are not taken, the pictures of the gathering in Geneva might become one of the last glimpses of sanity in our region." President Carter told the audience, "It is unlikely that we shall ever see a more promising foundation for peace. The only alternative to this initiative is sustained and permanent violence."

They are right. The formal launch of the Geneva Accord constitutes both a remarkable opportunity and a profound danger. If the Israeli people or the Palestinian people (or both) were to reject the only possible negotiated solution, then "sustained and permanent violence" would become the dire reality. The stakes have just been raised, and the moment of truth is at hand. Either both peoples will be winners or both will continue to be losers. The rest of the world must help Israelis and Palestinians to make the right choice, not only for their sake but for the sake of all of us.

TO ACHIEVE TWO STATES, ASK FOR ONE

PUBLICATIONS:

January 11, 2004 – Al-Quds (Jerusalem)
January 11 – Asharq Al-Awsat (London)
January 12 – Arab News (Jeddah)
January 12 – Jordan Times (Amman)
January 15 – Al-Ahram Weekly (Cairo)
January 16 – Jerusalem Times
January 17 – Daily Star (Beirut)
January 18 – Sunday Mail (Nicosia)
January 23 – Jerusalem Times (expanded version)

With Israeli Prime Minister Ariel Sharon threatening to impose the permanent status solution of his choice unilaterally if the Palestinians do not bow to his wishes within the next few months, Palestinian Prime Minister Ahmed Qurei has now responded with a quiet threat of his own which is far more likely than either continued violence or continued immobility to produce the sensible two-state solution which clear majorities of both Israelis and Palestinians wish to achieve.

In an interview on January 8, Qurei noted that the wall being built through the West Bank, which Sharon has pledged to complete notwithstanding overwhelming international opposition, represents an "apartheid solution" which would "put Palestinians like chickens in cages" and "kill the two-state vision". His conclusion? "We will go for a one-state solution. There is no other solution." On January 11, he reaffirmed this view as he stood before the wall.

The timing could not be better. The non-governmental Geneva Accord signed on December 1 has revealed, in meticulous detail, what any negotiated two-state solution would have to look like. No negotiated agreement which could conceivably be acceptable both to most Israelis and to most Palestinians could be more than very marginally different from the Geneva Accord, which contains all the fundamental substantive compromises long recognized to be necessary in any negotiated two-state solution. If such a two-state solution is simply not good enough for either Israelis or Palestinians, then only two alternative solutions remain – a one-state solution and a military solution.

In a one-state solution, the entire territory of the former Palestine Mandate would form a single democratic state, free of any form of discrimination based on race, religion or national origin and with equal rights for all who live there, as in any true democracy.

In a military solution, the most likely sequence of events, extending over a period of time which might last decades or be relatively brief, would be a completion of the ethnic cleansing of the indigenous population of historic Palestine (an option which is widely supported in Israeli public opinion polls), followed by a nuclear attack on Israel by one or more Muslim states which eventually acquire such weapons and an immediate, massive Israeli nuclear response against the Muslim world. This nightmare scenario is not alarmist. It is realistic in the absence of peace.

All indications are that, in the absence of another major expulsion of Palestinians to relieve the "demographic threat", Israeli public opinion would reject with horror the prospect of a single democratic state "from the sea to the river" which would be free of any form of discrimination and with equal rights for all who live there, considering such a state, rightly, as a complete negation of Zionism and of Israel's reason to exist. Indeed, the immediate response from Sharon adviser Zalman Shoval was that Qurei "may just as well call for a Palestinian state on the moon". The whole world must reject with horror the military solution and, with this in mind, help Israelis and Palestinians to make a better choice.

In these circumstances, the Palestinian leadership has both a desperate need and a rare opportunity to seize the initiative and change the agenda in a constructive way. It should now follow up on Qurei's broad hints with a clear ultimatum

70

that, if the Israeli government has not commenced government-to-government negotiations toward a two-state solution on the basis of the Geneva Accord by a fixed, near-term date, the Palestinian Authority will dissolve itself, returning to Israel full responsibility for administering and financing all aspects of life in the occupied territories, and the Palestinian leadership and people will thereafter seek, peacefully, "one man, one vote in a unitary state", to adopt the old slogan of the South African anti-apartheid movement. Even the United States would have difficulty opposing a peaceful demand for "one man, one vote". The long-running game of stringing out forever a perpetual "peace process" while further entrenching the occupation with new "facts on the ground" would finally be over. Faced with such a challenge, the current Israeli government, already wobbly, would almost certainly collapse, opening the way to its replacement by a new government genuinely interested in peace. A decent peace for both Israelis and Palestinians would suddenly be possible, even close.

The road to peace based on a two-state solution is not a straight one. As the Palestinian leadership appears now to realize, the expressway to this destination is, in fact, a bypass road permitting Israelis to focus clearly on the one-state alternative and, now that the precise terms of any two-state solution have been revealed, to embrace those terms as, at least, the lesser evil and make the changes in their own leadership which would finally bring the Israeli-Palestinian conflict to an end.

"TERRORISM": A WORLD ENSNARED BY A WORD

PUBLICATIONS:

February 18, 2004 – International Herald Tribune (Paris)
February 18 – Gulf Times (Doha)
February 19 – Al-Ahram Weekly (Cairo)
February 23 – Al-Quds (Jerusalem)
February 23 – Jordan Times (Amman)
February 27 – Jerusalem Times

In his televised "Meet the Press" interview on February 8, President George W. Bush was never asked a question about "terrorism". Yet, in his answers, he used the word (or a variant) 22 times. This word explained, and justified, everything – past, present and future.

Few American politicians or commentators dare to question the conventional wisdom that "terrorism" is the greatest threat facing America and the world. If so, the real threat lies not in the behavior to which this word is applied but, rather, in the word itself.

It is no accident that there is no agreed definition of "terrorism", since the word is so subjective as to be devoid of any inherent meaning. At the same time, the word is extremely dangerous, because people tend to believe that it does have meaning and to use and abuse the word by applying it to whatever they hate as a way of avoiding rational thought and discussion and, frequently, excusing their own illegal and immoral behavior.

There is no shortage of precise verbal formulations for the diverse acts to which the word "terrorism" is often applied. "Mass murder", "assassination", "arson" and "sabotage" are available (to all of which the phrase "politically motivated" can be added if appropriate), and such crimes are already on the statute books, rendering specific criminal legislation for

72

"terrorism" unnecessary and undesirable.

However, such precise formulations do not carry the overwhelming, demonizing and thought-deadening impact of the word "terrorism", which is, of course, precisely the charm of the word for its more cynical and unprincipled users and abusers. If someone commits "politically motivated mass murder", people might be curious as to the cause or grievance which inspired such a crime, but no cause or grievance can justify (or even explain) "terrorism", which, all right-thinking people must agree, is the ultimate evil.

Most acts to which the word "terrorism" is applied (at least in the West) are tactics of the weak, usually (although not always) against the strong. Such acts are not a tactic of choice but of last resort. To cite one example, the Palestinians would certainly prefer to be able to fight for their freedom from a 36-year-long occupation by "respectable" means, using F-16's, Apache attack helicopters and laser-guided missiles such as those the United States provides to Israel. If the United States provided such weapons to Palestine as well, the problem of suicide bombers would be solved. Until it does, or at least until the Palestinians can see some hope for a decent future, no one should be surprised or shocked that Palestinians use the "delivery systems" available to them – their own bodies. Genuine hope for something better than a life worse than death is the only cure for the despair which inspires such gruesome violence.

The poor, the weak and the oppressed rarely complain about "terrorism". The rich, the strong and the oppressors constantly do. While most of mankind has more reason to fear the high-technology violence of the strong than the low-technology violence of the weak, the fundamental mind-trick employed by the abusers of the epithet "terrorism" is essentially this: The low-technology violence of the weak is such an abomination that there are no limits on the high-technology violence of the strong which can be deployed against it.

Not surprisingly, since September 11, 2001, virtually every recognized state confronting an insurgency or separatist

73

movement has eagerly jumped on the "war on terrorism" bandwagon, branding its domestic opponents (if it had not already done so) "terrorists" and, at least implicitly, taking the position that, since no one dares to criticize the United States for doing whatever it deems necessary in its "war on terrorism", no one should criticize whatever they now do to suppress their own "terrorists". Even while accepting that many people labeled "terrorists" are genuinely reprehensible, it should be recognized that neither respect for human rights nor the human condition is likely to be enhanced by this apparent carte blanche seized by the strong to crush the weak as they see fit.

Perhaps the only honest and globally workable definition of "terrorism" is an explicitly subjective one – "violence which I don't support". Anyone who reads both the Western and Arab press cannot help noticing that the Western press routinely characterizes as "terrorism" virtually all Palestinian violence against Israelis (even against Israeli occupation forces within Palestine), while the Arab press routinely characterizes as "terrorism" virtually all Israeli violence against Palestinians. Only such a formulation would accomodate both characterizations, as well as most others.

If everyone recognized that the word "terrorism" is fundamentally an epithet and a term of abuse, with no intrinsic meaning, there would be no more reason to worry about the word now than prior to September 11. However, with the United States relying on the word to assert, apparently, an absolute right to attack any country it dislikes, many people around the world understandably feel a genuine sense of terror (dictionary definition: "a state of intense fear") as to where the United States is taking the rest of the world.

Meanwhile, in America itself, the Bush administration has for the past two years been feeding the U.S. Constitution and America's traditions of civil liberties, due process and the rule of law (the finest aspects of American life and the principal reasons why the country used to be respected abroad out of admiration and not simply out of fear) into a shredder. Who would have imagined that 19 men armed only with knives and box-cutters could accomplish so much, provoking a response, beyond their wildest dreams, which has proven vastly more damaging to their enemies even than their own appalling acts? Some sense of proportion, and some reflection on the real dimensions of "terrorism" (and even of September 11), is in order. It was not inevitable that the events of that day, awful though they were, would "change the world forever". In an average three-day period, more Americans die from smoking than were killed in the September 11 attacks. That is a serious problem. In an average month, more Americans die from gunshots inflicted by their fellow Americans than were killed in the September 11 attacks. That is a serious problem. AIDS is a serious problem. Global warming is a serious problem. Even if an attack of September 11 dimensions occurred every few months, "terrorism" would still be a lesser problem than these and many other problems facing America and the world.

If the world is to avoid a descent into anarchy, in which the only rule is "might makes right", every "retaliation" provokes a "counter-retaliation" and a genuine "war of civilizations" is ignited, the world – and particularly the United States – must recognize that "terrorism" is simply a word, a subjective epithet, not an objective reality and certainly not an excuse to suspend all the rules of international law and domestic civil liberties which have, until now, made at least some parts of our planet decent places to live.

The world – and particularly the United States – must also recognize that, in a world filled with injustice, violent outbursts by those hoping desperately for a better life or simply seeking to strike a blow against injustice or their tormentors before they die can never be eradicated. At best, the frequency and gravity of such outbursts can be diminished by seeking to alleviate (rather than continuing to aggravate) the injustices and humiliations that give rise to them. A single-minded focus on increased military, "security" and "counter-terrorism" programs and spending will almost certainly continue to prove counter-productive to its declared objective, diminishing both security and the quality of life for all mankind. Perfect security is, and will always be, an illusion, and "victory" in a "war on terrorism" is no more likely than in a "war on poverty", a "war on crime" or a "war on drugs".

It is long overdue, but not too late, for the American people to liberate themselves from the aggressive and self-destructive paranoia inflicted on them by unscrupulous abusers of an undefinable word. Perhaps John Kerry will have the courage and genuine patriotism to question the wisdom of continuing to wage a perpetual "war" against a subjective epithet and, by doing so, to set us free, restoring some measure of sanity and more mature and constructive priorities both to American society and to America's relations with the world.

A MOMENT TO PAUSE AND REFLECT

PUBLICATIONS:

March 18, 2004 – Gulf Times (Doha)
March 20 – Cyprus Mail (Nicosia)
March 22 – Arab News (Jeddah)
March 23 – Jordan Times (Amman)
March 25 – Al-Ahram Weekly (Cairo)
May 2004 – Washington Report on Middle East Affairs
Spring 2004 – GOAB-Bulletin (Vienna)
Spring 2004 – International (Vienna)

The gruesome train bombings in Madrid and the stunning regime change which followed should be seized upon to rethink whether the "war on terrorism", as conceived and conducted since September 11, 2001, is really the most effective way to deal with a problem that shows no signs of going away.

If a patient is ill, a doctor who misdiagnoses the source and nature of the illness and prescribes a course of treatment for a different disease risks killing the patient. After two and a half years of a "war on terrorism" which is widely perceived in the Middle East as an expansion of a long-running Western war against Muslims or, worse, as a Judeo-Christian crusade against Islam, it is worth reconsidering whether the initial diagnosis and the subsequent treatment are more likely to kill the patient than to save him.

Americans are notoriously ignorant of, and uninterested in, history – even very recent history. Only in America could President George W. Bush say, after the conquest of Iraq and more than once, that he invaded Iraq because it would not let UN weapon inspectors back into the country and not trigger any serious questions as to his fitness for office, even from his political opponents.

Accordingly, Americans have tended to view the September 11 attacks as a bolt from the blue, inexplicable, based on pure malevolence and carried out by people willing to sacrifice their lives out of an incomprehensible, irrational and incurable fanaticism unconnected to any concrete grievances or goals. Few Americans have dared to suggest that, however awful the attacks were, they might have constituted a response or a reaction to policies which the United States (or Israel, widely viewed by Muslims – and, apparently, by most Americans – as indistinguishable from the United States) has pursued in the region.

The immediate American response to such appalling violence was to resort to superior violence, and the continuing American reaction to the fear instilled by the attacks has been to try to instill a still greater fear in potential adversaries. This has proven to be a "bleeding" cure for an anemic patient.

Viewed from the region, Muslims have been subjected to a century of conquest, colonization, occupation and humiliation at the hands of Christians, Jews and the West. It started toward the end of World War I with the secret Sykes-Picot treaty, by which Britain and France carved up between themselves the most historic and sophisticated portion of the Arabian peninsula, which they had told their Arab allies they were "liberating" from the oppressive Ottomans, and the Balfour Declaration, by which Britain promised to give away Palestine, which did not belong to it. It has continued with the expulsion or flight into exile of most of the Palestinians in 1948, the catastrophic war of June 1967, the fall of Baghdad last spring and numerous other humiliations along the way.

The Muslims possess no "respectable" or "socially acceptable" way to fight back. They cannot invade, rocket or send their air forces to attack Western countries. The only tactic available is "terrorism". If such "terrorism" were properly understood to be a brutal (but not irrational) reaction to a century of conquest, colonization, occupation and humiliation, and if the desire of Western politicians were really to diminish "terrorist" threats to the West, rather than simply to sustain and exploit them for personal political advantage or to faciliate the implementation of pre-existing agendas, then surely the worst possible approach would be (as it has been) to increase and intensify precisely these sources of frustration and fury through further conquest, colonization, occupation and humiliation. Wise and prudent people seek to assuage, not aggravate, legitimate grievances – and even grievances whose legitimacy they may not accept. The instinctive Israeli and American attitude is that halting or reversing the policies of conquest, colonization, occupation and humiliation would be to "reward terrorism". Perhaps, but if, by assuaging grievances, both injustice and terrorism could be diminished and the world could be made more livable and less frightening, would this not be the preferable alternative? In current circumstances, doing the right thing, however belatedly and with whatever motivation, simply makes self-interested sense. The Spanish electorate seems to have grasped this.

In this context, the currently proclaimed American intention, potentially to be supported by the Europeans, to "remake the face of the Middle East" – explicitly to make the region less threatening to America and implicitly to make it less threatening to Israel – promises, if pursued, to be spectacularly counterproductive.

Viewed from the region, particularly by those with access to Western media, it is also easy to get the impression (not irrationally) that, in Western eyes, Jewish and Christian lives are of infinite value while Muslim lives are of no value whatsoever. It is worth recalling in this regard that in December 1996, while U.S. ambassador to the UN, Madeleine Albright stated publicly that she considered the premature, sanctions-induced deaths of over 500,000 Iraqi children, as reported by UNICEF, a "price worth paying" for America's Iraq policy. This statement provoked no outrage in America. Indeed, a month later, she became secretary of state.

Needless to say, the deaths of somewhat fewer than 3000 Americans were far too high a price to pay for America's entire Middle East policy – an event which "changed the world forever" and has been used to justify the killing of many more than 3000 Afghans and many more than 3000 additional Iraqis, the occupation of two more Muslim countries and the destruction of fundamental rules of international law painfully developed over more than a century. This is not a course of action likely to win hearts and minds.

If the West truly wishes to restrain the violent Muslim reaction to Western behavior, the West must change its behavior. It must take seriously the principle for which the United States once purported to stand – that all men are created equal and endowed with inalienable rights – and start treating Muslims (particularly the long abused Palestinians) like human beings entitled to basic human rights.

The problem of "terrorism" can be viewed as a moral issue, a scourge toward which no effort at understanding is conceivable and shock, awe and overwhelming force are the only possible response. This approach has been tried for two and a half years. It has failed, and there is no reason to believe that "more of the same" will succeed.

Alternatively, the problem could be viewed as a practical one. What is most likely to "work", to reduce the violence, which can never be totally extinguished, to tolerable levels? The West could make a serious and sustained effort to reduce the injustices which feed the fury which produces the "terrorism", starting with the cancerous, 37-year-long occupation of Palestine. This approach has not yet been tried. It should be.

Since September 11, the United States has been dragging the world in precisely the wrong direction, one guaranteed to make an already ugly and dangerous situation even worse. Realistically, particularly in an election year, one cannot expect America to take the lead in changing course. Might Europe, which is both more aware of history and closer to the Middle East, take inspiration from the Spanish elections and lead the world in the right direction?

The world is at a crossroads. This should be a moment to pause, to reflect seriously on the abyss which lies before us and to ask with open minds whether there is not a better way forward.

LIFE AND DEATH IN SAUDI ARABIA

PUBLICATION:

June 3, 2004 – International Herald Tribune (Paris)

Saturday's bloody attacks on foreigners in Al-Khobar, the center of Saudi Arabia's oil industry, were apparently carried out by four young men. The attackers were methodical, efficient and, up to a point, even polite. They asked potential victims their religion and, if satisfied that they were Muslims, asked where they could find Americans.

While, extraordinarily, three escaped during an overnight siege, all must have expected to die and were clearly prepared to do so. Indeed, the ultimate security problem facing Saudi Arabia today may be finding a way to make life more attractive than death for young Saudi Arabian men. It will not be easy.

For the great majority of young Saudi Arabian men, who are not rich, life is truly grim. Even speaking to young girls can, literally, produce a lashing, and they may not be able to afford a wife. They cannot enjoy a beer with friends in a pub or bar. (There are none.) They cannot go to a disco. (There are none.) They cannot go to a movie theater. (There are none.) They cannot go to a concert. (There are none.) Even the physical aspect of this country is grim. They are not surrounded by beauty. In addition, given the country's staggering birth rate and unemployment rate, they are unlikely to find a job – or, at least, one providing any interest or satisfaction.

What *can* young Saudi Arabian men do? Essentially, two things. They can watch television, which, every day, shows them vivid and appalling images of Zionists and Crusaders killing, brutalizing or otherwise humiliating Muslims (true images, unfortunately), and they can wholeheartedly embrace their country's mandatory and austere interpretation of Islam, which emphasizes that this life is inconsequential in comparison with the "next life" to come, except in terms of assuring by one's acts the best possible place in the "next life", in which places of honor, and the most attractive living conditions, are reserved for "martyrs".

As psychologists know, arguments for suicide are more compelling to young people than to their elders, because the young still tend to think "magically" about the future. For frustrated young men facing thwarted lives without pleasure or hope, a spectacular death can seem a magical escape. Aspiring Muslim martyrs can believe that it will lead directly to a paradise whose sumptuous and erotic pleasures are the classic fantasies of adolescent dreams.

Young people do not need to be Saudi Arabian, Muslim or even religious to be tempted by a magical suicidal solution to their problems, but the unusual social and religious environment of Saudi Arabia and the intensification of the long-running Israeli and Western practices of conquest, colonization, occupation and humiliation of which Muslims are so visibly the victims combine to make young Saudi Arabian men particularly prone to this tragic temptation.

The preferred ways to seek martyrdom are currently to die fighting for the liberation of Palestine or Iraq against the Zionist and Crusader occupations. A respected, gray-bearded Saudi Arabian friend, who was born in Iraq, has been approached in mosques by children as young as ten seeking his help to infiltrate them into Iraq so that they can die fighting the Americans. He tries to discourage them, but, as he freely admits, the young no longer pay attention to members of his generation, held in contempt (even by their own sons and daughters, whose worldviews fill them with fear) for their perceived impotence in not fighting back against Israel and America.

However, the country's borders are closed. The only alternative for most of those seeking martyrdom is therefore to do so while striking a blow against "evil" at home. "Evil" is, of course, a subjective concept, but those in the Middle East or in America who view the world in terms of "good" and "evil" have the utmost confidence that they know it when they see it and that God is on their side. In Saudi Arabia, "evil" looks like me –

or like the representatives of a Saudi regime widely perceived as more concerned about pleasing people like me than about pleasing its own people.

What might make life more attractive than death for young Saudi Arabian men? The twin occupations of Palestine and Iraq – and the related humiliations of Muslims – might end through successful resistance, restoring a shared sense of dignity, self-respect and pride to Muslims. Or Saudi Arabian society might turn away from religion, with people increasingly focused on living this life decently (even pleasantly) for its own sake. Neither seems likely in the near term.

In these circumstances, attacks such as those in Al-Khobar and, a few weeks earlier, in Yanbu are not surprising. What is surprising is that they have not occurred more often. There is every reason to expect such attacks to continue and to increase in frequency, limited only by the availability of the means to carry them out, not by the numbers or the intensity of the rage, hate and yearning for a better life in another world of young men with the will to strike a blow and die.

AN ELEGANT EXIT FROM IRAQ

PUBLICATIONS :

September 30, 2004 -- Al-Ahram Weekly (Cairo)
October 1 – Asharq Al-Awsat (London)
October 1 – Jordan Times (Amman)
October 4 – Arab News (Jeddah)
October 7 – Courrier International (Paris)
October 10 – Sunday Mail (Nicosia)
November 2004 – Washington Report on Middle East Affairs

With polls showing that only two percent of Iraqis consider Americans "liberators" while solid majorities favor an immediate withdrawal of all American forces, a degree of skepticism as to the genuine eagerness of George W. Bush and Iyad Allawi to see free and fair elections held in January is understandable. There is a widespread assumption in the region that these elections will be postponed or, if held, will be rigged to ensure that any "sovereign" Iraqi government remains effectively subservient to American control.

However, genuinely free, fair and early elections may offer the United States the best, if not the only, hope for a relatively elegant escape from the deep hole which it has dug for itself in Iraq.

To seize this opportunity, Americans must come to grips with four hard truths which will be difficult to accept but, if accepted, could set them (and, not incidentally, the Iraqis) free.

First: America is not hated throughout the Arab world because "we love freedom" but because of America's policies in the Arab world. Prior to the Six-Day War of 1967 and America's subsequent unconditional embrace of Israel, Americans loved freedom no less, but the Western country hated in the Arab world was France. It was France which was brutalizing Algerian freedom fighters, invading Egypt (with its British and Israeli allies) to seize the Suez Canal, serving as Israel's principal arms supplier and helping to build Israel's nuclear bomb-building facility at Dimona. By contrast, the United States, which had told the invaders of Egypt to get out or else, was genuinely popular in the Arab world. After 1967, American and French policies changed, and Arab attitudes changed accordingly. If American policies changed again, this time for the better, so would Arab attitudes.

Second: Resistance to the occupation will continue as long as the occupation continues – or until Iraqis are convinced that the Americans really do intend to leave and to do so soon. With the United States continuing to build 14 "enduring bases" in Iraq and with its political leaders speaking (in total contempt of any concept of a "sovereign" Iraqi government) of keeping American troops in Iraq for another four years (John Kerry), another 20 years (John McCain) or as long as it takes to get the job done (most of the Bush administration), Iraqis can be forgiven for believing that the United States had no "exit strategy" because it never intended to leave, planning instead a military presence in Iraq as long-lasting as those in Germany, Japan and Korea. In these circumstances, any acts intended to convince the occupiers that the cost of staying is too high – even those deemed barbaric in the West – are apt to be viewed by most Iraqis as both justified and patriotic.

Third: No Iraqi government could long survive after the withdrawal of American forces without earning patriotic (hence anti-American) credentials, either from prior resistance, from its role in achieving American withdrawal or from subsequent anti-American policies. This will be equally true whether America withdraws next month or after another 20 years of occupation.

Fourth: A "democratic" government is one which accurately reflects the will of the governed. A "democratic" government is not automatically pro-American, pro-Israeli or pro-market. Indeed, in current circumstances, any "democratic" government in the Arab world would be strongly anti-American and anti-Israeli. Iraq is no exception.

Once these hard truths are absorbed, the light at the end of the tunnel comes into view. This is the scenario:

– Truly free and fair elections are held, producing a new Iraqi government which accurately reflects the will of the Iraqi people.

– This new government promptly asks the United States to withdraw all its troops within a fixed, relatively short period – say, three to six months.

– The United States, in compliance with the "democratically expressed will of the Iraqi people", agrees to do so and takes immediate, visible steps to demonstrate that it is doing so.

– The United States also promises to contribute massive reconstruction aid to Iraq over a sustained period of years after its withdrawal, such aid to be paid directly to the Iraqi government to spend as it sees fit, as is American aid to Israel. (Truly massive aid would cost much less than maintaining American forces – and be much more appreciated.) If Iraq chooses to characterize this aid as "reparations", the United States should not object. It would go without saying (and should not be said) that the United States could cut off this aid at any time if it deemed Iraqi policies too anti-American. Given the destitute condition of the Iraqi economy and infrastructure after years of war, sanctions and occupation, any Iraqi government would have a strong interest in behaving in a manner which kept this money flowing.

– More quietly, asylum in the United States is offered to all members of the American-appointed Governing Council and interim government and all other prominent Iraqis who have cooperated with the Americans and are, therefore, viewed as collaborators by their fellow Iraqis. This is the decent and honorable thing to do. (Israel opened its border to the collaborationist South Lebanon Army and their families after it withdrew its occupation forces from Lebanon.) This should also avoid gruesome scenes such as those of the charred bodies of "contractors" in Falluja.

– Simultaneously, the United States initiates and sustains a vigorous and determined effort to actually achieve peace in Israel and Palestine, an effort explicitly based on international law and justice, two concepts which have been absent from American involvement with this conflict since 1967 but which are essential to any solution. If this scenario played out, most of those engaged in violent resistance in Iraq would have nothing left to resist against. The new Iraqi government would be viewed as liberators rather than collaborators, and few would wish to risk slowing down the American withdrawal. Some current hardcore jihadists, in Iraq and elsewhere, would continue to seek martyrdom by striking a blow against evil (as they see it), but finding new recruits to the cause would become difficult. Today's broad sea of Arab and Muslim support for violent resistance to America would dry up. America would no longer be widely perceived, as it is today, as leading a Judeo-Christian crusade against Islam and Muslims, and the world would become a vastly less grim and frightening place in which to live than it is today.

It is difficult to imagine this scenario playing out if George W. Bush is reelected. In light of his public pronouncements, it is not easy to imagine it playing out if John Kerry is elected. Still, it is not an impossible scenario. Realistically, is there a better one?

"TERRORISM": THE WORD ITSELF IS DANGEROUS

This article is an expanded version of the op-ed article with the same title, first published in December 2001, which was commissioned by the quarterly journal *Global Dialogue* (Nicosia) for its Spring 2002 issue focused on the repercussions of September 11. It was also published in Spanish in the March/April 2002 issue of *Politica Exterior* (Madrid), in German in the Spring 2002 issue of *International* (Vienna) and, in booklet form, by the *Society for Austro-Arab Relations,* and in English in the June 2002 issue of the *Pugwash Newsletter,* the semiannual magazine of the Council of the Pugwash Conferences on Science and World Affairs (winner of the Nobel Peace Prize in 1995). In September 2002, it was posted on the official website of the U.S. Democratic Party ("www.democrats.com/view.cfm?id=9520").

The greatest threat to world peace and civil society today is clearly "terrorism" – not the behavior to which the word is applied but the word itself. Since the word "terrorism" (like the behavior to which the word is applied) can never be eradicated, it is imperative to expose it for what it is – a word.

For years, people have recited (often with a wry smile) the truisms that "One man's terrorist is another man's freedom fighter" and that "Terrorism, like beauty, is in the eye of the beholder". However, with the world's sole superpower declaring an open-ended, worldwide "war on terrorism", proclaiming that this "war" has only just begun and promising to persevere until "victory", the notorious subjectivity of this word is no longer a joke.

It is no accident that there is no agreed definition of "terrorism", since the word is so subjective as to be devoid of any inherent meaning. At the same time, however, the word is extremely dangerous, because many people tend to believe that it does have meaning and many others use and abuse the word by applying it to whatever they hate as a way of avoiding and discouraging rational thought and discussion and, frequently, excusing their own illegal and immoral behavior.

There is no shortage of precise verbal formulations for the diverse acts to which the word "terrorism" is often applied. "Mass murder", "assassination", "arson" and "sabotage" are available (to all of which the phrase "politically motivated" can be added if appropriate). However, such precise formulations do not carry the overwhelming, demonizing and thought-deadening impact of the word "terrorism", which is, of course, precisely the charm of the word for its more cynical and unprincipled users and abusers. If someone commits "politically motivated mass murder", people might be curious as to the cause or grievances which inspired such a crime, but no cause or grievance can justify (or even explain) "terrorism", which, all right-thinking people must agree, is the ultimate evil.

Crimes such as "murder", "arson" and "sabotage", as well as assorted gradations of them, are already on the statute books, rendering specific criminal legislation for "terrorism" as such both unnecessary and undesirable. Creating distinct crimes and punishments for "terrorist" offenses injects a wholly subjective element into criminal law, which, to be fair and to be seen to be fair, should be based rigorously on *what* a person has done, not *why* he did it (let alone who he is or to whom he did it). A crime labeled "terrorism" is almost always punished more severely than the same act to which the label "terrorism" is not attached. Thus, killing to advance a cause in which one deeply believes is deemed more reprehensible than killing because one dislikes the victim or wants to steal his property. One can understand why those in power might consider the former motivation more dangerous. The moral and ethical balance between the two motivations is less clear.

Any dispassionate analysis of the use of the word "terrorism" also reveals that the choice to use or not to use the word is frequently based not on the act itself but on who is doing it to whom. Prior to Israel's withdrawal of its occupation forces from southern Lebanon, French Prime Minister Lionel Jospin, on a visit to the region, used a press conference to publicly denounce as "terrorist acts" attacks by Hezbollah fighters against Israeli occupation forces within Lebanon. Mr.

Jospin seemed genuinely surprised when, the next day, Palestinians showered him with stones as he left a meeting with President Yasser Arafat in Ramallah. He should not have been surprised.

Mr. Jospin would never have dreamed of characterizing as "terrorist acts" attacks by French resistance fighters against German occupation forces in France during the Second World War. Such fighters are France's greatest heroes. Yet, objectively, there is no distinction between the two resistance struggles. The only distinction is who is resisting whom – a distinction blindingly clear to an Arab or Muslim audience. Mr. Jospin, a fundamentally decent man, surely did not intend to give a demonstration of racism and bigotry at his press conference. For someone raised in the West, where anti-Arab racism is the only socially acceptable form of racism (indeed, where it is almost obligatory at the highest levels of society), where Islamophobia is a deeply entrenched historical and social phenomenon and where anti-Arab and anti-Muslim propaganda is relentless and rarely questioned, it just came naturally.

Arabs and Muslims are acutely aware of the widespread Western (and particularly American) tendency to view them as less than fully human – or at least not as human beings entitled to basic human rights. Enthusiastic Western (and particularly American) approval of the transformation of the Arab land of Palestine into the Jewish state of Israel (necessarily requiring the dispossession and dispersal of the indigenous Palestinian population) and Western (and particularly American) indifference to the sanctions–induced premature deaths of over half a million Iraqi children under the age of five (characterized by former Secretary of State Madeleine Albright, without eliciting any discernible outrage in the United States, as a "price worth paying" for America's Iraq policy) cannot otherwise be explained. No one who believes that Arabs are human beings could approve of the former or be indifferent to the latter. Holding both views simultaneously is logically and intellectually impossible.

Arab and Muslim awareness of their dehumanization in

Western eyes, an obvious factor in enflaming the deep sense of humiliation and the white-hot hatred which produced both the September 11 attacks and the discreet but pervasive sense of satisfaction among Arabs and Muslims that someone had finally hit back, can only be further enflamed by the West's almost exclusive use of the demonizing term "terrorism", particularly since September 11, to refer to causes deemed just by most Arabs and Muslims. Even when the adjective "Islamic" is omitted, it seems to be implied and understood.

Americans in particular should not fool themselves about the true Arab and Muslim reaction to the September 11 attacks and the reason for that reaction. On January 30, 2002, the *Arab News*, Saudi Arabia's leading English-language newspaper, published the following report on an interview given to the *New York Times* by Saudi Arabia's Director of Intelligence, Prince Nawaf bin Abdul-Aziz Al-Saud: "Prince Nawaf acknowledged that the vast majority of Saudi young adults felt sympathy for the cause of Osama bin Laden after September 11... A classified U.S. report taken from a survey of educated Saudis between the ages of 25 and 41 in mid-October concluded that 95 percent of them supported bin Laden's cause.... He attributed the support to people's feelings against the U.S., largely because of its unflinching support of Israel."

Wars are waged against countries and people, not against religions or subjective epithets, but a "war on terrorism" whose targets are almost exclusively Muslim can readily be perceived by those so targeted and demonized, with potentially catastrophic results, as not simply a war against Muslims but a "war against Islam". A "war on terrorism" which brands virtually all efforts by Arabs and Muslims to right deeply felt wrongs as not just illegitimate but criminal, and which treats Arabs and Muslims generally as inherently suspect of "terrorist" intent and as unworthy of basic human rights, is virtually guaranteed to produce more and worse instances of precisely what this "war" is ostensibly intended to eradicate.

Most acts to which the word "terrorism" is applied (at least in the West) are tactics of the weak, usually (although not always) against the strong. Such acts are not a tactic of choice but of last resort. To cite one prominent example, the Palestinians would certainly prefer to be able to fight for their freedom from a never-ending occupation by "respectable" means, using F-16's, Apache attack helicopters and laser-guided missiles such as those the United States provides to Israel. If the United States provided such weapons to Palestine as well, the problem of suicide bombers would be solved. Until it does, or at least until the Palestinians can see some genuine and credible hope for a decent future, no one should be surprised or shocked that Palestinians use the "delivery systems" available to them – their own bodies. Genuine hope for something better than a life worse than death is the only cure for the despair which inspires such gruesome violence.

In this regard, it is worth noting that the poor, the weak and the oppressed rarely complain about "terrorism". The rich, the strong and the oppressors constantly do. While most of mankind has more reason to fear the high-technology violence of the strong than the low-technology violence of the weak, the fundamental mind-trick employed by the abusers of the epithet "terrorism" (no doubt, in some cases, unconsciously) is essentially this: The low-technology violence of the weak is such an abomination that there are no limits on the high-technology violence of the strong which can be deployed against it.

Not surprisingly, since September 11, virtually every recognized state confronting an insurgency or separatist movement has eagerly jumped on the "war on terrorism" bandwagon, branding its domestic opponents (if it had not already done so) "terrorists" and, at least implicitly, taking the position that, since no one dares to criticize the United States for doing whatever it deems necessary in *its* "war on terrorism", no one should criticize whatever they now do to suppress their own "terrorists". Even while accepting that many people labeled "terrorists" are genuinely reprehensible, it should be recognized that many others are idealists motivated by thoroughly legitimate grievances not susceptible to remedy by non-violent means and that neither respect for human rights nor the human condition is likely to be enhanced by this apparent *carte blanche* seized by the strong, in a sort of "unholy alliance" of all established regimes, to crush the weak as they see fit.

Writing in the *Washington Post* on October 15, 2001, Post Deputy Editor Jackson Diehl cited two prominent examples of the abuse of the epithet "terrorism": "With their handshake in the Kremlin, Sharon and Putin exchanged a common falsehood about the wars their armies are fighting against rebels in Chechnya and the West Bank and Gaza. In both cases, the underlying conflict is about national self-determination: statehood for the Palestinians, self-rule for Chechnya. The world is inclined to believe that both causes are just.... Sharon and Putin both have tried to convince the world that all their opponents are terrorists, which implies that the solution need not involve political concessions but merely a vigorous counter-terrorism campaign."

Perhaps the only intellectually honest and globally workable definition of "terrorism" is an explicitly subjective one – "violence which I don't support". This definition would explain the universal condemnation of "terrorism" in a world which, apparently, is full of it. By definition, you cannot support what you don't support, while, as a matter of usage, if *you* support it, it cannot be "terrorism". Indeed, anyone exposed to both Western and Arab media and public discourse cannot help noticing that Western media and public discourse routinely characterize as "terrorism" virtually all Palestinian violence against Israelis (even against Israeli occupation forces within Palestine), while Arab media and public discourse routinely characterize as "terrorism" virtually all Israeli violence against Palestinians. Only such an explicitly subjective formulation would accommodate both characterizations, as well as most others.

However, the word has been so devalued that even violence is no longer an essential prerequisite for its use. In December 2001, a Saudi Arabian lawyer told the press while announcing a multi-billion-dollar lawsuit against ten international tobacco companies: "We will demand that tobacco firms be included on the lists of terrorists and those financing and sponsoring terrorism because of the large number of victims that smoking has claimed the world over." (On the level of relative moral culpability, this is not an absurd concept. More Americans are killed by cigarettes in an average three-day period than were killed in the September 11 attacks. Moreover, the tobacco industry kills for financial gain, not, like more traditional "terrorists", in the hope of making the world, at least by their own subjective standards, a better place.)

If everyone recognized that the word "terrorism" is fundamentally an epithet and a term of abuse, with no intrinsic meaning, there would be no more reason to worry about the word now than prior to September 11. However, with the United States relying on the word to assert, apparently, an absolute right to attack any country it dislikes (for the most part, countries Israel dislikes) and with President Bush repeatedly menacing that "either you're with us or you're with the terrorists" (which effectively means, "either you make our enemies your enemies or you'll be our enemy – and you know what we do to our enemies"), many people around the world must feel a genuine sense of terror (dictionary definition: "a state of intense fear") as to where the United States is taking the rest of the world.

Meanwhile, in America itself, the Bush administration appears to be feeding the U.S. Constitution and America's traditions of civil liberties, due process, the rule of law and fundamental fairness (the finest aspects of American life and the principal reasons why the country used to be respected out of admiration and not simply out of fear) into a shredder – mostly to domestic applause or acquiescence. Centuries-old civil liberties have suffered a similar fate in the United Kingdom, for no apparent reason other than an irresistible inclination to follow the United States blindly in everything it does. Who would have imagined that 19 angry men armed only with knives could accomplish so much, provoking a response, beyond their wildest dreams, which threatens to be vastly more damaging to their enemies even than their own appalling acts?

The transformation of the Taliban, in American terminology and consciousness, from a particularly backward and repressive government (so regarded by most Muslims as well) to a regime "harboring terrorists" and, finally, to "terrorists" of the worst sort is a dramatic example of the threats to international law, common sense and enlightened national self-interest inherent in the casual, even sloppy, use of the word "terrorist".

It should be recalled that, soon after September 11, the United States demanded that Afghanistan hand over Osama bin Laden. This ultimatum came not only with a stick (the promise of attack and overthrow in the absence of compliance) but also, at least implicitly, with a carrot (the promise of not being attacked in the event of compliance). Had bin Laden been handed over, one must assume that the Taliban would still be going about their business of governing Afghanistan rather loosely and badly.

Afghanistan asked for evidence, none was forthcoming and the United States attacked. Prior to the attack, although the United States has long had very inclusive lists of "terrorist organizations" and "states supporting terrorism", neither the Taliban nor Afghanistan had figured on those lists. Yet, imperceptibly but rapidly, and without it even being alleged that a single Afghan citizen had prior knowledge of the September 11 attacks, anyone associated in any way with the Taliban – politically, administratively, as a simple soldier and even as Ambassador to Pakistan – became a "terrorist", to be "smoked out", "run to ground" and killed if possible and "brought to justice" if, unfortunately, he surrendered before he could be killed. The United States stated publicly that it was not interested in taking prisoners or in having its hastily recruited Afghan allies do so, a stance which itself constitutes a war crime.

On December 5, 2001, the *Arab News* published a letter to the editor from this writer which read: "U.S. Defense Secretary Donald Rumsfeld is reported to be demanding 'physical custody' of all Taliban leaders and as saying 'his legal staff was studying the question of how to try the Taliban chief, Mulla Muhammad Omar ... and other senior figures' from the Taliban. Perhaps 'What for?' would be a more relevant question than 'How?' It is not difficult to imagine criminal charges being leveled against Al-Qaeda leaders, although there seems to be no confidence in the Bush administration that such charges would hold up in an open court with normal due process protections for defendants. But what is the 'crime' of the Taliban leaders? Refusing to extradite a resident to a country with which their country had no extradition treaty? Resisting (ineffectively) an American attack against their country? Conspiracy to murder the CIA agent caught up in the Qalai Janghi prison massacre? Is this the sort of 'justice' for which the whole world is supposed to rally unquestioningly behind the United States?"

Well into 2002, the question "How?" was still being asked, though principally about simple soldiers, since few Taliban leaders had been captured. Are they to be tried by a secret American military tribunal? By a conventional American court martial? By an American civilian court? By a court in Afghanistan or the Taliban soldier's country of origin? The question "What for?" was still not being asked. Presumably, were it to be asked, the answer would be obvious: "Terrorism". Since these miserable soldiers are now deemed "terrorists", it is apparently irrelevant that the United States attacked Afghanistan, not the other way around, and that they never even had a chance to fight back, simply being subjected to massive aerial bombardments until they either were killed or surrendered. As "terrorists", they must surely be guilty of *some* heinous crime and surely have no claim to any rights whatsoever.

In this context, there is something almost psychedelic about the case of John Walker Lindh, the 20-year-old "American Taliban" whose conversion to Islam and search for some greater meaning in life than that offered by the self-centered consumerism of the "American dream" led him to the wrong place at the wrong time, to being bombed by American military forces, barely surviving the Qalai Janghi prison massacre after surrendering, being returned to the United States in chains and being indicted (potentially subject to life imprisonment although not, despite considerable public support for it, to the death penalty) for (believe it or not) "conspiracy to kill Americans". ("Conspiracy" is, of course, the charge traditionally leveled in the United States against people who didn't actually *do* anything but whom prosecutors are determined, for whatever reason, to convict.)

On January 23, 2002, the *International Herald Tribune* published a letter to the editor from this writer which read: "The United States contends that the Taliban fighters it is holding in open-air cages at its Cuban naval enclave are not 'prisoners of war' entitled to the rights and protections of the Geneva Conventions, but merely 'unlawful combatants' entitled to no rights at all in a place specifically selected because no law applies there. If the United States is justified in this contention, it follows logically that the world's only superpower has attacked a country which was one of the poorest on earth and whose regime possessed no military forces, making the U.S. 'victory' in Afghanistan more worthy of ethical embarrassment than patriotic pride."

Seemingly intoxicated by the concept of waging a worldwide war against "terrorists" and culturally programmed to view Arabs and Muslims as less than fully human, the United States, by its treatment of those captured in Afghanistan, had managed to restoke the fires of resentment and hatred in Arab and Muslim countries to levels even higher than prior to September 11, to sacrifice the moral high ground in countries neither natural allies nor natural enemies and to cause public opinion even in countries as fervently pro-American as the United Kingdom to publicly question what sort of country the United States has become. As Robert Fisk wrote in *The Independent* (London) in late January 2002: "Congratulations, America. You have made Osama bin Laden a happy man.... We are turning ourselves into the kind of deceitful, ruthless people whom bin Laden imagines us to be. We are now the very model of the enemies bin Laden wants to fight. He must be a happy man." Such assistance as other countries may continue to offer to the United States in its "war on terrorism" will increasingly be offered out of fear or cynical self-interest rather than out of any genuine conviction.

If the world is to avoid a descent into anarchy, in which the only rule is "might makes right", every "retaliation" provokes a "counter-retaliation" and a genuine "war of civilizations" is ignited, the world – and particularly the United States – must recognize that "terrorism" is simply a word, a subjective epithet, not an objective reality and certainly not an excuse to suspend all the rules of international law, domestic civil liberties and fundamental fairness which have, until now, made at least some parts of our planet decent places to live.

The world – and particularly the United States – must also recognize that, in a world filled with injustice, violent outbursts by those hoping desperately for a better life or simply seeking to strike a blow against injustice or their tormentors before they die can never be eradicated. At best, the frequency and gravity of such outbursts can be diminished by seeking to alleviate (rather than to aggravate) the injustices and humiliations that give rise to them, by more consistent and universal application of the fundamental religious principle to "do unto others as you would have others do unto you" and of the fundamental principle of the founding fathers of American democracy that all men are created equal and endowed with inalienable rights, by treating *all* people (even one's enemies) as human beings entitled to basic human rights and by striving to offer hope and human dignity to the miserable millions who have neither. A single-minded focus on increased military, "security" and "counter-terrorism" programs and spending will almost certainly prove counter-productive to its declared objective, diminishing both security and the quality of life not only for the poor, the weak and the oppressed but also for the rich, the strong and the oppressors.

The trend since September 11 has been to aggravate, rather than to alleviate, the very problems which fueled the sense of humiliation and hatred behind that day's attacks.

However, it is not inevitable that this trend must continue – unless, of course, men and women of good will, compassion and ethical values, who share a well-founded fear as to where the world is heading and can see clearly that there must be, and is, a better way, permit themselves to be terrorized into silence.

A BRIEF HISTORICAL REFLECTION

PUBLICATION:

September 26, 2002 – The Times (London)

During the 1930's, a great country went completely off the rails. Through democratic elections (albeit with only a minority of the popular vote), a clique of extreme right-wing ideologues came to power. They sincerely believed that their vision of a better world was destined to triumph over all alternative visions. They considered their country exempt from all constraints of international law and treaty obligations. They sought to dominate the world, seizing opportunities or excuses to attack other countries and impose their will by force. They repressed civil liberties at home and treated certain ethnic and religious groups, both at home and abroad, as sub-humans unworthy of basic human rights. They fanned the flames of ultranationalism, making their flag a sort of fetish and a virtual object of worship.

Either out of genuine enthusiasm or out of fear of being branded "unpatriotic", the great majority of their fellow citizens either supported these arrogant and dangerous delusions or kept their silence. Few dared to speak out and say that their country was headed in a direction that was both unworthy of its heritage and better values and potentially catastrophic. It turned out very badly, both for Germany and for the world.

At the start of the 21st century, will the people of another great country prove to be "good Germans"? Or will they dare to speak out, before it is too late, against the unworthy and potentially catastrophic direction in which their regime is taking them? If current trends continue, it will turn out very badly, both for America and for the world.

Five and Ten Press Inc.

This is a small, independent press that publishes quality (in content, not necessarily in presentation) paperback original works of fiction, non-fiction, and our specialty "factual fiction," in a variety of genres: memoirs, essays, short stories, novellas, miscellanies, even (once) poetry. All are published in limited first editions of from 300 to 600 copies, in 5" by 8" format that makes them convenient to carry in a coat pocket or purse while traveling on one conveyance or another. They rarely exceed 100 pages in length, so are not heavy to read in bed. The print font is fairly large, easy on the eyes.

Known as "Black Sheep Books," they are always priced at between $5 and $10, hence the name of the press. They are sold individually from our website (fiveandtenpress.com), by internet booksellers such as amazon.com, and most successfully by subscription. Subscribers, of whom there are now around 200, pay the press $25 in advance and receive, sight unseen, the next three or four publications. There are never any annoying charges for "shipping and handling," which for other presses are disguised profit centers. We mail by first class postage, which guarantees delivery.

Despite our stringent editorial quality control, we have thus far been able to publish 23 booklets. Ten have been authored by Robert V. Keeley, but we have also published ten other writers. The main criterion for publication is that the manuscript must show some wit, if possible a lot of wit. And secondly originality. Also, needless to say, readable style (not just "style"). Essentially we publish what mainstream (that is, commercial) publishers, magazines, newspapers, journals, and other outlets have no interest in and usually don't bother to respond to efforts to interest them.

If you would like to subscribe, just send us a check for $25 and make sure you enclose your mailing address. If you would like to buy individual copies, here is our list, with prices shown. There are no discounts, and no charges for postage. New subscribers receive a free "signing bonus" copy of their choice of any of these publications.

Five and Ten Press Inc.
3814 Livingston Street N.W.
Washington, D.C. 20015-2803

Black Sheep Books--1995-2004

By Robert V. Keeley:

1. **D.C. Governance: It's Always Been a Matter of Race and Money.** 29 pages. December 1995. Second printing February 1996. $5. (Out of print. Photocopy only.) The fundamental problem of the nation's capital and a possible solution.

2. **Annals of Investing: Steve Forbes vs. Warren Buffett.** 49 pages. March 1996. $5. Second printing May 2000. Black humor. How not to--and how to--make money in the stock market.

3. **The File: A Princeton Memoir.** 96 pages. May 1996. $10. Nostalgia. Undergraduate escapades three decades--and many other changes--after F. Scott Fitzgerald.

4. **Essays Fast and Loose: A Christmas Miscellany.** 76 pages. November 1996. $7. The O.J. Simpson case solved, corporate culture criticized, health care reformed, the Olympics put down, Colin Powell questioned, Forbes revisited, and dancing for free cruises.

5. **Letters Mostly Unpublished.** 72 pages. March 1997. $5. Twenty-two items, mostly letters to the editor, most--and some of the best--of which never got into print.

6. **Essays Cold and Hot: A New Year's Potpourri.** 95 pages. January 1998. $10. Two terrible Supreme Court decisions, the condition of the nation's capital, a dysfunctional Senate, Andreas Papandreou of Greece, how to cure the common cold, and a Hollywood fantasy.

7. **MSS Revisited.** 72 pages. April 1998. $7. A Princeton undergraduate literary magazine recalled, with short stories by Jose Donoso, Walter Clemons, and R. V. Keeley.

8. **Three Sea Stories.** 102 pages. October 1999. $10. Memoirs. Lessons learned by a 16-year-old on a merchant marine voyage, by a 24-year-old on U.S. Coast Guard weather patrol, and by a 29-year-old in an encounter with a hospitalized sea captain.

9. **The Great Phelsuma Caper (A Diplomatic Memoir).** 140 pages. December 2000. $10. Macabre adventures with General Idi Amin Dada of Uganda, toilet training a pet bird, smuggling lizards, and other tall tales.

10. **Essays Near and Far: As a New Century Dawns.** 124 pages. April 2002. $10. Nine new essays on diplomacy and foreign relations: civility in diplomacy, relations with Greece, Balkans turmoil, Israel-Palestine, defining terrorism, Nelson Mandela.

By other authors :

11. **Innocents of the Latter Day: Modern Americans Abroad.** 98 pages. May 1997. $10. By James W. Spain, a retired American ambassador. Eleven short stories about the Foreign Service set in South Asia, the Near East, and Africa.

12. **Creatures of the Earth and the Mind.** 60 pages. October 1998. $6. By Carl Coon, a retired American ambassador. Nine charming stories and essays about animal life, plus a profound essay about concepts underlying progressive humanism.

13. **My Commute.** 76 pages. December 1998. $10. By Alison Autobound Axel. Novella. A humorous, insightful account of contemporary corporate life from the point of view of a denizen of a cubicle at a large multinational to which she commutes daily. Dedicated to the downsized.

14. **Sic Transit.** 68 pages. December 1999. $6. By Carl Coon. Thirteen essays, some satirical, some humorous, some serious. Topics include power, the military mind, foreign affairs, Morocco, Nepal, marital relations, gender and generational differences, New York City, the Pope, and cyberspace.

15. **Poetry Mostly Off The Beaten Track.** 56 pages. May 2001. $5. By Roy Herbert. A course in understanding poetry, citing great poems of the past. Includes some unpublished poems by the author.

16. **Random Thoughts, Anecdotes, and Memories of a Boys' Latin School of Baltimore That Is No More.** 25 pages. Illustrated. January 2004. $5. By Don Hahn. The period is 1935-47. The author is a medical doctor in Mendocino, California, a graduate of Princeton, where he was a legendary star in lacrosse, and of Johns Hopkins. His father was headmaster of the school.

17. **From The Heartland.** 101 pages. Maps included. February 2004. $10. By Carl Coon. A memoir of his service as U.S. Consul in Tabriz, Iran. Followed by 'From Osh to Lhasa,' a travelogue of a 1993 exploration through large parts of Central Asia, Chinese Turkestan, and Tibet.

18. **One of the Very Best Men.** 56 pages. Illustrated. March 2004. $5. By Robert Sherwood Dillon. A memoir of post high school years from 1946 to 1956, at college in Virginia, as an enlisted man in the U.S. Army, as a CIA operative involved in paramilitary operations off the coast of China, and later on Taiwan, before joining the Foreign Service, where he served as ambassador to Lebanon.

19. **A Story Goes With It.** 63 pages. June 2004. $7. By George Garrett. A shotgun wedding of fact and fiction, this tells one version of the tale of Nazi saboteurs who landed in America, in both Florida and Long Island, early in 1942. An almost comic and slapstick disaster, this terrorist attack came close to succeeding, because the American authorities reacted with equal ineptitude and matching inefficiency. An unusual event in our nation's history, retold with verve, humor, and foreboding.

20. **Low Crimes and Misdemeanors in High Places: John Mitchell and Watergate.** 51 pages. November 2004. $5. By Edmund Keeley. A thoroughly-researched reexamination and retelling of the Watergate scandal focused on the role of John Mitchell, President Nixon's former law partner, his attorney general, and manager of his 1972 re-election campaign. Mitchell became the fall guy, went to prison, but didn't save Nixon from resignation and disgrace.